BEFORE

YOU

LEAVE

What walking away will cost you

RAKIEM JAMAL

Copyright © 2025 Rakiem Jamal
All rights reserved.

No part of this book may be reproduced, stored in a retrieval system, or transmitted in any form or by any means—electronic, mechanical, photocopying, recording, or otherwise—without the prior written permission of the author, except for brief quotations in reviews or articles.

Contents

CHAPTER ONE: THE HOPPER 1

CHAPTER TWO: THE BLAMER 13

CHAPTER THREE: THE ATTENTION SEEKER 26

CHAPTER FOUR: THE ABUSED 34

CHAPTER FIVE: THE REJECTED 44

CHAPTER SIX: THE BLEEDING LEADER 54

CHAPTER SEVEN: THE CONFUSED 63

CHAPTER EIGHT: THE INDEPENDENT SPIRIT 73

CHAPTER NINE: THE OFFENDED 84

CHAPTER TEN: WHAT WAS THE REASON THAT YOU STARTED? ... 94

CHAPTER ELEVEN: THE BENEFITS OF FAITHFULNESS 104

CHAPTER TWELVE: TIME FOR A RESET 109

CHAPTER THIRTEEN: IT'S TIME TO GO! 130

FINAL WORDS & CONCLUSION 139

Foreword

The average human being makes about **35,000 decisions** a day. Many of these decisions are made without much thought—automatic, routine, and often without seeking God's guidance. Yet, decisions shape our lives and can alter the course of our destiny.

Have you ever planned to go somewhere but, for some reason, decided against it—only to later hear that something terrible happened there? In that moment, you instinctively say, **"Thank God I didn't go!"** If we recognize His hand in protecting us in those small, unspoken moments, how much more should we involve God in the weightier decisions of life—such as leaving a church or walking away from a ministry?

Before You Leave is not just another book; it is a lifeline. It is a call to pause, reflect, and ensure that your decision is not based on fleeting emotions, temporary frustration, or circumstantial discomfort. The decision to leave is not just about you—it has the potential to affect your entire generation.

Maybe you're holding this book in your hands, uncertain about whether to stay or go. Maybe you're flipping through these pages to decide if this book is even worth reading. Let me assure you—**there is a reason you picked up this book.** You need to read it.

Prophet Rakiem Jamal understands the power of making **God-centered decisions** and the discipline required to submit to His voice—even when it's difficult, even when it contradicts personal desires, even when it costs something. This book is not written to condemn you or point fingers. It is not about anyone in particular, yet at the same time, it is about everyone—because we all make decisions.

Before You Leave was written to **empower, equip, and edify you.** How do I know this? Because the author is my husband.

And I've watched him live out every word.

— Prophet Rakiem's Wife

CHAPTER ONE: THE HOPPER

Confessions of a Church Hopper: The Story of Sarah

Sarah was well-known in many churches, not because of her leadership or spiritual depth, but because she was everywhere. She hopped from church to church, conference to conference, always chasing the next big spiritual event. She had been in so many places that people stopped taking her seriously. They recognized her face but never saw her stay long enough to grow.

One day, Sarah joined a small, biblically grounded church pastored by a humble man of God. He noticed her pattern early on and warned her about the dangers of church hopping. "Sarah," he told her, "not every well is pure, and not every place that calls itself a church is of Christ. You need to be planted where God has called you, or you will find yourself drinking from contaminated wells."

But Sarah found his words controlling. She confided in some church members, telling them that her pastor was too rigid. "All churches are Christian, right? Why should it be a problem where I go? If God is moving, I should be free to experience Him anywhere," she reasoned.

Though Sarah enjoyed the wisdom her pastor shared, she felt something was missing. Every time she scrolled through YouTube, she saw videos of preachers performing miracles—casting out demons, healing the sick, and commanding supernatural encounters. It stirred something in her. "Why doesn't my pastor do these things?" she wondered. Soon, she lost interest in her local church and set her sights on something more exciting.

An opportunity arose for her to attend a major deliverance conference in Nigeria, where thousands gathered to witness the power of God. The videos looked intense—people were screaming, spirits were manifesting, and the atmosphere was electric. Without hesitation, Sarah booked her flight, convinced that this experience would bring her closer to God.

When she arrived, the reality was even more extreme than what she had seen online. People in her row were vomiting, convulsing, and screaming as demons were "cast out." The energy in the room was overwhelming. But as Sarah lifted her hands in surrender, something strange happened—she lost control. Instead of being delivered, she felt a darkness enter her. Her body shook violently, and an unfamiliar voice came out of her mouth. Sarah had unknowingly opened herself up to a spirit she was never meant to encounter.

Days later, she returned home, but she was no longer the same. Her mind was tormented. She couldn't sleep, and when she did, she had terrifying visions. She would hear voices calling her name, feel invisible hands gripping her at night, and experience unexplained fits of rage. The joy and peace she once knew were gone.

Years passed, and Sarah became a shadow of herself. She isolated from others, ashamed of what had happened. She sought help in different churches, but people either dismissed her or were too afraid to pray for her. The same church leaders she had once chased after now ignored her, leaving her trapped in her torment.

One day, a friend invited her to a local conference. Although skeptical, desperation pushed her to attend. As she entered, something about the atmosphere felt familiar. Then she saw the speaker—it was her former pastor, the one she dismissed as "too simple."

That night, he preached with such power and conviction that Sarah couldn't escape the weight of his words. As he began to pray, something inside her reacted violently. She fell to the ground, vomiting uncontrollably as the spirit that had tormented her for years was finally cast out.

The same pastor she had left in search of "greater things" was the one God used to restore her.

Sarah's story is a painful reminder that chasing supernatural experiences without discernment can lead to spiritual destruction. Not every manifestation is from God, and not every gathering that claims Christ is holy. Had she remained planted where God had assigned her, she would have avoided years of torment.

Not every church is safe. Not every preacher is sent by God. And not every spiritual experience leads to freedom. The question is—are you seeking a deeper walk with God, or are you chasing the next big thing?

Who Is the Hopper?

The Hopper is someone who never stays rooted. They attend a church for a season, but as soon as conflict arises, the excitement fades, or discomfort sets in, they move on. Initially, they tell themselves it's about "finding the right fit," but eventually they realize—the cycle never ends.

They may have visited multiple churches without ever staying long enough to build spiritual roots. They start new relationships, ministries, and assignments—but never commit long enough to truly grow.

Here's the dangerous part: Hopping is often disguised as spiritual hunger, when in reality, it frequently indicates spiritual instability.

Profile of the Hopper

- Do you frequently change churches, whether after a few months or a few years?
- Are you quick to find mistakes in the church you attend?
- Do you struggle to trust church members and church leaders?
- Do you avoid conflict resolution and prefer to leave rather than confront it?
- Are you constantly searching for an emotional or spiritual high rather than consistent growth?
- Have you left multiple churches over disagreements or disappointments?
- Do you see church involvement more as an experience rather than a place of commitment?
- Do you believe people should visit churches or conferences whenever they feel like it?

If you found yourself answering yes to several of these, you may be struggling with a Hopper mindset. Recognizing this pattern is the first step to embracing true spiritual stability.

Root Causes & Biblical Insights

1. **Chasing Emotional Highs Instead of Spiritual Growth**
   Many believers confuse goosebumps with growth. If a church doesn't give them the same spiritual "rush" they once had, they assume something is wrong.

   Biblical Insight:
   - **2 Timothy 4:3** – "…they will gather around them a great number of teachers to say what their itching ears want to

hear."

True spiritual maturity isn't measured by how many services you attend, but by how deeply you are transformed.

2. **Avoiding Correction and Accountability**

   Some believers leave not because God led them out, but because correction made them uncomfortable.

   Biblical Insight:
   - **Hebrews 12:11** – "No discipline seems pleasant at the time… later it produces righteousness…"
     If you run whenever you feel convicted, you'll never grow. True transformation happens when you stay planted long enough for God to refine you.

3. **Lack of Trust in Church Leadership**

   Many Hoppers have been hurt by leaders and now don't trust anyone to lead them.

   Biblical Insight:
   - **Hebrews 13:17** – "Obey your leaders and submit to them… they keep watch over your souls…"
     Being planted doesn't mean surrendering to man—it means submitting to God's order.

4. **The Fear of Commitment & Process**

   Many Hoppers love new beginnings but fear long-term commitment.

   Biblical Insight:
   - **Psalm 92:13** – "Those who are planted in the house of the Lord shall flourish."
     Commitment means staying even when emotions fade, showing up when it's inconvenient, and growing through hard seasons rather than running from them. God never called you to "explore" the Church—He called you to **build** it.

Reflections & Questions

1. Have you ever found yourself constantly moving from one church to another? If so, why?
2. What are you truly looking for in a church?
3. How can you cultivate spiritual stability in your current church?
4. Do you leave at the first sign of discomfort, or do you allow yourself to grow through challenges?
5. What does "being planted" mean to you, and how can you apply that to your faith journey?
6. **James 1:8** – "A double-minded man is unstable in all his ways." How does this verse apply to church hopping?
7. **Colossians 2:7** – "Let your roots grow down into Him." What does it mean to be deeply rooted in Christ?
8. **Psalm 1:3** – "They are like a tree planted by streams of water, which yields fruit in season." How does being planted connect with bearing fruit?

Breaking the Cycle of Church Hopping

1. **Recognize the Pattern**
   Be honest about your frequent moves. Are you avoiding growth, running from correction, or chasing emotions over true maturity?
2. **Make a Commitment to Stay**
   Decide to be planted and grow spiritual roots, even when it's uncomfortable. Lasting growth requires consistency, not constant movement.
3. **Heal from Past Church Hurts**
   Don't let past disappointments define your future. Seek healing, forgive, and move forward with a renewed heart.

4. **Embrace Accountability**
   Surround yourself with trusted believers or mentors who can guide, encourage, and keep you on track.
5. **Refocus on Purpose**
   Shift from being a consumer to a contributor. Instead of seeking a perfect church, ask God how you can serve and build where He has placed ou.

PROPHETIC DECLARATIONS

- I break free from every cycle of instability in Jesus' name!
- I refuse to be uprooted before my time—I will stay where God plants me!
- I reject the deception that tells me to follow emotions instead of God's process!
- Psalm 92:13 – "I declare that I am planted in the house of the Lord, and I SHALL FLOURISH!"
- I receive the grace to submit to godly leadership and grow in humility!
- I embrace correction, knowing that it will refine me for my next level!
- Where God has assigned me, I will stay! I will not abort my destiny!
- I receive endurance to remain faithful through every test and trial!
- James 1:4 – "I declare that perseverance will finish its work in me, making me mature and complete!"

The 3-Step Hopper Challenge

If you're serious about breaking the cycle of hopping, consider this challenge:

Step 1: Find an Accountability Partner

Let them know you struggle with church hopping, and ask them to check in on your progress.

Why This Helps:

- Encouragement & Motivation: They can remind you of your commitment.
- Honest Feedback: A good partner will lovingly correct you when you're making excuses.
- Shared Wisdom: They may have overcome similar struggles.
- Spiritual Support: They can pray for you and help you stay aligned with God's will.

How to Make It Work:

- Be honest about your struggle.
- Set clear check-in times (weekly or daily).
- Allow them to challenge you when you're off track.
- Celebrate each milestone together, no matter how small.

Step 2: Make the Above Declarations for 7 Days

Words carry power. In the Kingdom, dominion is often voice-activated. Until you begin to **speak** life, true transformation may remain elusive.

Why Declarations Matter:

1. They renew your mind (Romans 12:2).

2. They shape your destiny (God spoke creation into existence).
3. They activate faith (Romans 10:17).
4. They enforce spiritual realities.
5. They shift your perspective.

How to Speak for Transformation:
- Dedicate time daily (morning and night).
- Personalize each declaration—make it your reality.
- Believe what you say—speak with authority.
- Be consistent for 7 days—repetition cements the truth in your spirit.

This isn't mere motivation; it's **spiritual legislation**. Open your mouth and prophesy your victory!

Step 3: Commit to 5 Months of No Hopping

"You cannot grow where you are not planted. If you keep moving, you will never mature." — Joshua Selman

"A tree that is constantly uprooted will never bear fruit. Stability is the key to spiritual growth." — Myles Munroe

The Call to Be Planted & Fully Committed

Many desire growth, anointing, and transformation but fail in one critical area—**stability**. One of the biggest hindrances to spiritual maturity is church hopping. Jumping from service to service, ignoring the place God has assigned you, is a sign of spiritual instability.

For the next 5 months, make a firm decision:
- No attending services outside your own church.
- No missing your church's gatherings.

- Be present for every service—Sunday, midweek, prayer meetings.
- Serve, stay accountable, and allow God to work in you where He planted you.

This isn't about restriction; it's about spiritual discipline. **You cannot be deeply rooted if you're constantly shifting**. Growth requires consistent nourishment in the environment God has chosen for you.

Why 5 Months of No Hopping?

1. **Spiritual Growth Requires Stability** – "Those who are planted in the house of the Lord shall flourish" (Psalm 92:13).
2. **God Blesses Order & Submission** – Rejecting God-ordained leadership or structure hinders your growth.
3. **You Miss Out on Your Own Growth** – Every outside service missed is a lost opportunity for what God might be doing in your home church.
4. **Hopping Breeds Confusion** – Receiving from too many unaligned sources can cause doctrinal and spiritual chaos.
5. **God Moves in Seasons** – There are things God wants to establish in you at your assigned church, but you must remain long enough to receive them.

Requirements for Commitment:

- No attending other revivals or conferences for 5 months—focus on your own church.
- Don't skip your church's services—Sunday or midweek.
- Submit to your leadership—allow pastors and mentors to shape you.
- Engage in serving—find a way to contribute to the work of God.
- Stay accountable—have your accountability partner ensure you're sticking to the plan.

What Happens When You Stay Planted for 5 Months?
- **You grow spiritually** – Depth comes from consistency.
- **You hear God clearly** – No more confusion from too many voices.
- **You develop discipline** – Stability is required for leadership and anointing.
- **You flourish in your calling** – God promotes those who remain faithful.
- **You break cycles of inconsistency** – The enemy thrives on distractions. This commitment counters that strategy.

A Contract with Yourself & God

Make this challenge a covenant:

"Lord, for the next 5 months, I commit to being planted where You have assigned me. I will not hop around. I will not miss my church's gatherings. I will serve, grow, and remain faithful. I surrender to Your process, knowing You are working in me for my good. In Jesus' Name, Amen!"

Signature: _____

Date: _____

Closing Prayer

Father, thank You for placing me in Your house. I repent for every time I ran to the next place instead of growing where You planted me. Uproot every restless desire in my heart. Give me the discernment to know Your voice, the humility to stay where I'm called, and the strength to endure when challenges arise. Help me to be rooted, stable, and committed, bearing fruit for Your kingdom. In Jesus' name, **Amen**.

Final Words

Are you a Hopper? Have you been running from process or correction?

Decide today to be planted. Stay long enough to let God shape you. Stay long enough to truly grow.

Before you leave—ask yourself: **Is God really leading me, or am I running from what I need to face?**

Remember, **breaking free from church hopping is a choice**. The moment you choose to be planted, you step into a transformative process leading to deep spiritual maturity and lasting fruitfulness.

CHAPTER TWO: THE BLAMER

Confessions of a Blamer: The Story of Andrew

Andrew had always been the rising star of his church—charismatic, passionate, and deeply knowledgeable of the Word. He was the kind of leader people naturally gravitated toward. Everywhere he went, people listened. When he spoke, people took notes. When he prayed, people cried. When he walked into a room, heads turned.

He wasn't just another church member—he was a movement. Everyone knew that one day, Andrew would become a powerful pastor. His calling was undeniable, and his fire was unmatched.

But the greater the admiration, the greater the expectation. And the greater the expectation… the greater the fall.

It all started with one sermon.

The Sermon That Shattered Everything

The sanctuary was full. The guest preacher stood tall behind the pulpit, his voice steady, his presence commanding. Andrew sat in his usual spot—front and center, surrounded by supporters.

Then it happened.

"There are some in this house," the preacher began, "who think they are bigger than the house itself. They gather people to themselves, not to Christ. They act like they love the church, but their loyalty is only to their own ego. And when they don't get the spotlight, they'll cause division and blame leadership."

A chill ran through the room. The preacher never said a name, but everyone knew who he was talking about.

Andrew sat rigid, jaw clenched, his pulse hammering. He could feel eyes shifting toward him, feel the silent whispers pressing in. His heart pounded against his ribs.

"Why isn't Pastor stopping this?"

The betrayal hit him in the chest. His pastor—his spiritual father—sat just a few feet away, watching. No interruption. No correction. No defense. The message continued, but Andrew wasn't listening anymore. His mind had already made a decision.

The Moment That Broke Him

After service, Andrew stormed into his pastor's office, body vibrating with rage.
"Did you hear what he said?!" he demanded.

His pastor sat behind his desk, expression unreadable. "I did."

"And you let that happen? You let him stand there and humiliate me in front of everyone?"

His pastor let out a slow breath. "Andrew… he never said your name."

Andrew's fists clenched.
"Don't play games with me!" he snapped. "Everyone knew he was talking about me! And you—you let it happen!"

His pastor studied him for a long moment.
"Andrew, I need you to take a step back and ask yourself something... was he wrong?"

The final blow. Andrew felt heat rise to his face.
"You're just like the rest of them," he hissed.

His pastor's expression remained calm. "Andrew, I understand why you're upset. But how you respond now will reveal everything."

But Andrew was done listening.

The Exodus That Shook the Church

Andrew left that day with fire in his veins. But he wasn't just leaving—he was taking people with him. He whispered in hallways about the corrupt leadership, sat in coffee shops planting seeds of doubt, and embellished the story until his betrayal became theirs.

"They tried to humiliate me. They let that preacher slander me from the pulpit!"

People believed him. People followed him. And when Andrew started his own church, many of those same people walked through his doors. "Here," he told them, "we will build a REAL church." For years, it looked like he had. Until the past came knocking on his door.

Ethan: The Shadow of His Own Mistakes

Ethan was one of Andrew's most promising young leaders—passionate, bold, and a lover of truth. Andrew saw himself in him. The church was thriving, and so was Ethan's influence. People admired his zeal, depth, and conviction. Andrew was proud of him.

But there was something else. Ethan had an edge—an impatience for weakness, a frustration for anything that felt like compromise. Then, just like before, it happened. A small misunderstanding between Ethan and another leader turned into something bigger. Ethan expected Andrew to step in and correct it. But Andrew, older and wiser now, tried to calm the storm instead of taking sides.

"Ethan, I hear you, but you need to handle this with grace."

Ethan's eyes burned.
"Handle this with grace? Is that what we do now?" he scoffed.

Andrew felt a chill.
"I thought we were different, Pastor. But you're just like them."

Andrew tried to reason with him, but Ethan had already made up his mind.

The Betrayal That Brought It All Full Circle

Ethan didn't just leave—he left loud. He posted about corruption in leadership, shared "exposing the truth" videos on social media, and whispered in small groups about how Andrew had let him down.

Andrew tried to fight back, but then his own wife spoke softly one night: "Andrew… isn't this exactly what you did?"

Suddenly, Andrew saw the truth he had never wanted to face. "What I have sown, I am now reaping." For the first time in years, Andrew bowed his head—not in pride or anger, but in humility. "God… forgive me." And for the first time since this all began, the cycle was broken.

Who Is the Blamer?

The Blamer struggles to take responsibility for their spiritual growth. They shift the focus onto others, believing their struggles are caused by leadership, the church, or circumstances. Instead of recognizing their own role in their spiritual journey, they develop a habit of pointing fingers.

Blamers often feel overlooked, unappreciated, or misunderstood. They become easily offended and hold onto past hurts, allowing bitterness to take root. However, the greatest danger of the Blamer mindset is that it keeps people stuck—unable to move forward in their faith because they believe the problem is external rather than internal.

If left unchecked, this mindset creates a cycle of frustration, isolation, and stagnation. But freedom comes when we recognize that our spiritual growth is our own responsibility, not something controlled by others.

Profile of the Blamer

- Do you often feel like your spiritual stagnation is due to how others treat you?
- Are you quick to criticize church leadership, ministries, and fellow believers?
- Do you frequently leave churches feeling misunderstood, hurt, or unappreciated?
- Do you believe that if others changed, your faith would be stronger?
- Have you found yourself repeating the same cycle of dissatisfaction in different churches?
- Do you struggle with correction and accountability, feeling like others are unfairly judging you?

- Do you sometimes feel resentful toward those who are thriving in their faith, assuming they had better opportunities?

If you answered yes to several of these, you may be struggling with the Blamer mindset. Recognizing this is the first step toward spiritual maturity and healing.

Root Causes & Biblical Insights

1. **Refusing Personal Responsibility for Spiritual Growth**
   Blamers tend to shift responsibility for their spiritual condition onto others. Instead of seeking personal transformation, they focus on external circumstances.
   Biblical Insight:
   - **Galatians 6:5** – "Each one should carry their own load."
     Your growth is your responsibility. No one else can seek God on your behalf.

2. **Unhealed Wounds Leading to Bitterness**
   Blamers often carry past hurt and allow it to shape their perception of leadership and community.
   Biblical Insight:
   - **Proverbs 19:3** – "A person's own folly leads to their ruin, yet their heart rages against the Lord."
     Bitterness blinds you to your own role in your situation. Healing comes when you release the past.

3. **Resistance to Correction & Accountability**
   Blamers see correction as an attack rather than an opportunity for growth.
   Biblical Insight:
   - **Matthew 7:3–5** – "Why do you look at the speck in your brother's eye and not notice the plank in your own?"
     Correction is not rejection—it's God's way of refining you.

4. **The Spirit of Entitlement**
   Some Blamers believe they deserve recognition or leadership roles without proving faithfulness. When overlooked, they become offended.
   Biblical Insight:
   - **James 1:22** – "Be doers of the word, and not hearers only, deceiving yourselves."
     God promotes those who serve with humility, not those who demand positions.

Reflections & Questions

1. Do I often blame others for my spiritual stagnation?
2. How do I handle correction and feedback?
3. Have I contributed to the issues I complain about?
4. What areas of my faith journey require self-reflection rather than external blame?
5. **Matthew 7:3–5** – How does this scripture challenge me to examine myself before blaming others?
6. **Hebrews 12:15** – "See to it that no one falls short of the grace of God and that no bitter root grows up to cause trouble and defile many." In what ways has bitterness affected my view of the church?

Breaking the Cycle of Blame

1. **Acknowledge Your Patterns**
   Recognize if you habitually blame others instead of taking responsibility for your own spiritual walk. Be honest about the excuses you make.

2. **Release the Past**
   Choose to let go of past hurts and allow God to heal the wounds that keep you stuck. Blame doesn't bring freedom; it only delays it.
3. **Accept Correction with Humility**
   View correction as an opportunity to grow, not an attack. True wisdom comes from a teachable spirit.
4. **Shift from Complaining to Serving**
   Instead of criticizing leadership or ministry, actively contribute and be part of the solution. If you see a problem, ask God how you can help fix it.
5. **Refocus on Your Assignment**
   Understand that your growth is your responsibility, not dependent on everyone else treating you perfectly. Let your faith be rooted in God, not in people's actions.

Breaking free from blame is a choice. The moment you accept ownership of your faith, you step into maturity, stability, and purpose.

PROPHETIC DECLARATIONS

- **I break free from the spirit of blame in Jesus' name!**
- **I take full responsibility for my spiritual growth and walk in maturity!**
- **Galatians 6:5** – "I carry my own load and take charge of my walk with God!"
- **I reject every root of bitterness and choose healing over offense!**
- **I receive correction with humility, knowing it refines my character!**
- **I silence every lying voice that tells me others are to blame for my struggles!**

- I will not let past wounds dictate my future in Christ!
- I declare that I am emotionally and spiritually stable!
- **Hebrews 12:15** – "I will not allow a bitter root to defile my heart!"
- I walk in humility, serve with joy, and trust God's process for my growth!
- The favor and blessings of God rest on me as I choose faithfulness over entitlement!
- I am a builder, not a destroyer. I uplift rather than blame!
- I declare that I am healed, accountable, and empowered in Jesus' name!
- _____

The 3-Step Blamer Challenge

Step 1: Find an Accountability Partner

"You will never change what you refuse to take ownership of." — Myles Munroe

The Power of Accountability

One of the easiest ways to remain stuck in blame is isolation. With no one checking your mindset, it's easy to justify blaming others. An accountability partner will challenge you to take responsibility instead of pointing fingers.

Why You Need an Accountability Partner:
1. **They Expose Your Blind Spots** – You may not realize how often you shift blame until someone points it out.
2. **They Challenge You to Grow** – When you try to blame others, they'll urge you to self-reflect instead.

3. **They Keep You Honest** – It's harder to justify your behavior when you have to report it to someone else.
4. **They Help You Walk in Maturity** – Growth thrives in community, not isolation.

How to Apply This Step

- Choose someone trustworthy who can be both honest and supportive.
- Tell them about your tendency to blame.
- Give them permission to correct you.
- Check in regularly—weekly or daily—to review your progress.

Blame is a prison, but accountability is the key. Let truth and correction transform you.

Step 2: Make the Above Declarations for 7 Days

Why Declarations Matter

The more you blame others, the more you reinforce a victim mentality. What you reinforce, you empower. If you want to break free, you must start speaking **truth** over yourself.

How to Apply This Step

- Recite the listed declarations every morning and night for 7 days.
- Personalize them—attach your name and specific struggles.
- Speak them aloud—faith comes by hearing, and the first ears to hear are your own.
- Be consistent—7 days of speaking life rewires your mindset and breaks the chains of blame.

Declarations aren't just words; they're spiritual laws shaping your reality. Open your mouth and prophesy your freedom.

Step 3: Commit to 5 Months of Self-Examination

"You will never master what you refuse to confront." — Myles Munroe

The Power of Self-Examination

Blame is easy; it avoids looking at yourself. Transformation requires courage to examine your actions, motives, and decisions.

For the next 5 months:
- **No blaming others.**
- **No shifting responsibility.**
- Each time you're tempted to blame, pause and ask: "What's my part in this?"
- Accept correction and learn from mistakes.

This isn't about guilt; it's about **growth**. If you don't reflect honestly, you'll keep repeating the same cycles.

Why 5 Months of Self-Examination?
1. **Awareness Sparks Change** – You can't change what you refuse to recognize.
2. **It Breaks the Blame Cycle** – Reflecting instead of reacting rewires your thought patterns.
3. **It Produces Spiritual Maturity** – God won't entrust you with more if you keep blaming others for your failures.
4. **It Forces You to Grow** – Comfort is the enemy of progress; self-examination keeps you challenged.

How to Apply This Step

- Keep a journal—record moments when you catch yourself blaming.
- Pause before reacting—ask, "What could I do differently?"
- Accept correction—stop justifying; start learning.
- Remain accountable—your partner (Step 1) should track your progress.

For 5 months, **no more blame**. Choose maturity, choose transformation.

A Contract with Yourself & God

This is more than a challenge—it's a **covenant** between you and God. If you accept, sign below:

"Lord, for the next 5 months, I commit to breaking free from blame. I will not shift responsibility. I will not live as a victim. I will examine my own actions and grow in maturity. I surrender to Your process, trusting You are shaping me for something greater. In Jesus' Name, **Amen!**"

Signature: _____

Date: _____

This is your breakthrough moment. No more blame, no more excuses—just transformation!

Closing Prayer

Father, in the mighty name of Jesus, I surrender every tendency to blame others for my struggles. I repent for every time I pointed fingers instead of looking inward. Let every stronghold of pride, every spirit of entitlement, and every seed of bitterness be uprooted in Jesus' name. Break the cycle of blame over my life. Teach me to walk in humility, embrace correction, and take responsibility for my faith. From today, I declare I am free. In Jesus' name, **Amen**.

Final Words

Are you a Blamer? Have you been blaming others for your spiritual struggles instead of owning your faith journey?

Decide today to walk in maturity, accountability, and self-examination. Before you leave—ask yourself: **Am I looking outward for the problem, or is God calling me to look within?** Embrace personal responsibility, and watch God transform your life from within.

CHAPTER THREE: THE ATTENTION SEEKER

Naomi: The Price of Seeking Attention

Naomi wasn't just a member of the church—she was the pastor's spiritual daughter. For years, she had served faithfully, pouring herself into ministry. She led prayer nights, coordinated worship rehearsals, and was entrusted with leading Bible studies. She had her pastor's trust, affirmation, and favor.

But not his wife's approval. No matter how much she dedicated herself to the ministry, she could never obtain the same favor from the pastor's wife.

Naomi could feel the distance. It wasn't hostility or jealousy—it was discernment. The pastor's wife saw what Naomi didn't want to admit: Naomi's service wasn't just devotion—it was hunger for recognition. She didn't just want to serve—she wanted to be seen.

Naomi knew it was true, but she buried it. Then Rachel arrived.

Rachel: The One Who Had Everything Naomi Wanted

Rachel wasn't trying to be seen or promoted; she was simply serving. Yet, somehow, Rachel was quickly noticed. She received opportunities Naomi had waited years for, was invited into meetings Naomi had long desired, and was publicly affirmed. Worst of all, Rachel was loved by the pastor's wife.

That was the final wound Naomi couldn't ignore. She felt her position slipping—her attention, favor, and validation. Something inside her broke: "If I can't have that favor... she won't either."

The Poison of Gossip

Naomi didn't plan an outright attack. She was too clever for that. She knew the best way to destroy someone wasn't to accuse them directly—it was to plant seeds:

- "I love Rachel, but don't you think it's strange how fast she's being promoted?"
- "I've seen Pastor spending extra time with her lately. I'm not saying anything... but have you noticed?"
- "I just pray that Rachel keeps her heart pure with all the attention she's getting..."

She never accused outright; she simply suggested. And suggestion is dangerous because people don't remember what was said—they remember what they assumed. Soon, Rachel's name was whispered in hallways. Doubt spread. Suspicion grew. Naomi watched from the shadows as Rachel's favor came into question.

The Guest Speaker & The Setup

One Sunday, the pastor called Naomi aside.
"Naomi, a guest speaker is coming next week. I want you to pick him up from the airport."
It wasn't the recognition she hoped for, but it was access, and she could work with that.

The Ride to the Airport

When Naomi picked up the well-respected minister, she dropped subtle hints about Rachel—how she was "very involved," how things had "changed" since she arrived. The minister filled in the rest. Naomi knew she had won. If she couldn't be the pastor's favorite, she would make sure Rachel wasn't either.

The Moment of Exposure

The church was packed that Sunday. The guest speaker was introduced with honor. Naomi sat smugly. Then, the pastor made a special announcement:

"Naomi has been one of my most faithful daughters. I am excited to announce she is being ordained as a minister!"

The room erupted with applause. Naomi stared, unable to move. Then she heard a sharp intake of breath behind her. She turned slowly.

The guest speaker's face was pale, his eyes locked onto hers—and she realized he was the one sent to ordain her.

Another voice spoke:
"Naomi, we have waited a long time for this moment."

She met the pastor's wife's eyes and saw warmth, approval, validation. Naomi had nearly destroyed it all.

Her legs gave out. She fell, weeping. Attention had cost her everything.

Naomi almost left the church in shame but chose healing over escaping. Her greatest mistake was trying to be seen by people when she was already fully known by God.

Who Is the Attention Seeker?

The Attention Seeker thrives on being in the spotlight. Their identity is wrapped up in recognition, applause, and acknowledgment. When they feel unseen or replaced, they struggle to stay committed. At its heart, attention-seeking is not just pride—it is misplaced identity. Rather than being anchored in God's love, Attention Seekers measure their worth by how much attention they receive.

Matthew 6:1 – "Be careful not to practice your righteousness in front of others to be seen by them."

If attention fuels your service, rejection will end it. A person who serves for human approval will walk away when that approval fades.

Profile of the Attention Seeker

- Do you feel discouraged when you aren't publicly recognized for your work?
- Do you feel that you should have been promoted for leadership or a greater position?
- Do you feel jealous when someone else is chosen for something you wanted?
- Do you struggle to celebrate others when they are promoted before you?
- Would you still serve faithfully even if no one ever acknowledged you?
- Do you feel tempted to leave when you feel overlooked?

If you see these traits in yourself, take it as an opportunity to realign your heart. Your worth is not determined by people's validation, but by God's unconditional love.

Breaking the Cycle of Attention-Seeking

1. **Recognize Where Your Validation Comes From**
   Your worth is found in Christ, not in human applause.
2. **Serve with a Pure Heart**
   Shift from "being seen" to "pleasing God."

3. **Stay Rooted in Humility**
   Avoid comparison, and embrace serving God whether or not people notice.
4. **Reject the Spirit of Competition**
   Ministry is not a race. Focus on your own growth and assignment.
5. **Anchor Your Identity in God**
   Your value lies in who you are in Christ, not in what people think of you.

Prophetic Declarations

- I reject the need for human validation—my identity is in Christ.
- I will serve with humility, knowing my reward is in heaven.
- I will not perform for applause—I will worship in surrender.
- I celebrate others without jealousy.
- I reject pride and insecurity in Jesus' name.
- I am rooted in God's purpose, not people's approval.
- I will serve faithfully, even in hidden seasons.
- I refuse to compare myself to others—I focus on my own race.
- My worth is in Christ, not in platforms or titles.
- God's promotion comes in His time, and I trust Him.

The 3-Step Attention Challenge

Step 1: Find an Accountability Partner

Why Accountability?

The addiction to recognition is subtle but dangerous. The enemy knows that if he can keep you seeking validation from people, you will never be fully surrendered to God.

Proverbs 27:17 – "As iron sharpens iron, so one person sharpens another."

How to Apply:

- Choose someone spiritually mature who can be honest with you.
- Share your struggle openly.
- Grant them permission to call you out when you slip into attention-seeking.
- Remain accountable, with regular check-ins.

Step 2: Make the Above Declarations for 7 Days

Why Declarations Matter

Attention-seeking begins in the mind. You must replace lies with truth. **Romans 12:2** – "Do not conform to the pattern of this world, but be transformed by the renewing of your mind."

How to Apply:

- Recite the listed declarations daily for 7 days.
- Speak them aloud, believing each word.
- Reflect on them throughout the day.

Speaking truth confronts the mindset at its root. Declare life until you believe it.

Step 3: Commit to 5 Months of Hidden Service

The Power of Serving in Secret

Jesus taught that giving in secret pleases God (Matthew 6:3–4). Serving in hidden roles kills the craving for recognition and purifies your motives.

How to Apply:

- Serve in a capacity where few people see you.
- Resist the urge to announce your service.
- Let your heart be refined by serving simply because God has called you.

A Contract with Yourself & God

"Lord, for the next 5 months, I commit to breaking free from attention-seeking. I will not serve for applause. I will not crave recognition. I will serve where only You see me, knowing that You are my reward. I surrender my desire to be seen, and I trust You to elevate me in Your time. In Jesus' Name, Amen."

Signature: _____

Date: _____

Closing Prayer

Father, I repent for every time I sought recognition instead of true worship. Break every root of pride, insecurity, and offense in my heart. Teach me to serve for Your glory alone. I surrender my need for validation and choose to worship You in spirit and truth. In Jesus' name, Amen.

Final Words

Are you an Attention Seeker? Have you placed more value on being seen than on being surrendered?

Decide today to serve with humility. Let go of pride, and trust God's timing. Before you leave—ask yourself: **Have I been seeking God's glory or my own?**

CHAPTER FOUR: THE ABUSED

Confessions of the Abused: The Story of Elijah

Elijah was a young man with a future most could only dream of. From a young age, he dedicated himself to soccer, pouring countless hours into training. He became a professional player, stepping into the career he had always wanted. But despite his success, something wasn't right. A whisper in his heart drew him to business and ministry—two areas he hadn't imagined pursuing.

After much prayer, Elijah made the most difficult decision of his life—he walked away from his soccer career. He invested his savings to build a business, but his real passion became serving in the church. With no family in town, the church became his home, his pastor became his spiritual father, and his resources became the church's resources.

What Elijah didn't realize was that the man he trusted most saw his sacrifice as an opportunity—and he would pay a heavy price for it.

The Pastor Who Took Advantage of Him

At first, Elijah admired his pastor—a strong leader, commanding speaker, a visionary. Elijah wanted to learn, to be mentored and discipled. The pastor welcomed him in.

"You're different, Elijah," he said. "God has big plans for you."

Those words meant everything to Elijah. He had given up so much for God, and his leader recognized him.

Elijah poured himself into ministry. He worked behind the scenes, never complaining, honoring his leader both in private and in public. He wanted to be faithful.

But faithfulness should never be blind.

Used for Financial Gain

It began subtly. The pastor asked Elijah to cover the bill when they ate out, borrowed his Mercedes, then borrowed money but never repaid.

"Son, the work of God is important. Sow into the kingdom, and you'll be blessed."

At first, Elijah saw it as an honor—he had resources, and his pastor had needs. But the requests turned into expectations. The pastor never paid for meals, hinted he wanted expensive gifts, and demanded Elijah's financial support for church projects.

"Elijah, you're blessed! Be a kingdom financier!"

The more Elijah gave, the less valued he felt. He wasn't being nurtured—he was being used.

From Honor to Control

It wasn't just about money. It was about power. Corrections were gentle at first, but over time, the pastor's tone changed:

- What once felt like mentorship now felt like control.
- What started as correction turned into public humiliation.
- What seemed like spiritual covering became manipulation.

If Elijah made a mistake, the pastor didn't correct him privately—he exposed him in front of the entire church.
"Some people in this house think they're humble, but they're full of pride," the pastor would say.

Elijah knew the remark was about him. That was the night he realized: this isn't breaking me to refine me; it's breaking me to destroy me.

Who Is the Abused?

The Abused are those who have been mistreated in church environments—spiritually manipulated, verbally abused, publicly shamed, or emotionally controlled. Some have experienced betrayal, neglect, or leadership that exploited their loyalty. These scars can affect one's ability to trust God's people.

Jeremiah 23:1 – "Woe to the shepherds who destroy and scatter the sheep…"
Spiritual abuse isn't just painful—it's dangerous to the soul.

Profile of the Abused

- Have you felt controlled rather than led in a church setting?
- Have you been publicly shamed or belittled by a spiritual leader?
- Do you struggle with trusting pastors or leadership because of past wounds?
- Have you felt obligated to serve, give, or obey out of fear?
- Have you left a church but still feel emotionally bound by what happened there?
- Do you experience anxiety or guilt when thinking about returning to church?

- Have you questioned your own worth because of mistreatment in ministry?

If you answered yes to several of these, you may be carrying wounds of spiritual abuse. Recognizing them is the first step toward healing.

Root Causes & Biblical Insights

1. **Corrupt Leadership Is Not of God**
   Ezekiel 34:4 – "You have ruled them harshly and brutally."
   God condemns spiritual leaders who manipulate and control.

2. **God Is a Healer, Not an Abuser**
   Psalm 147:3 – "He heals the brokenhearted and binds up their wounds."
   God is not the author of your pain; He is the One who will heal you.

3. **Church Should Be a Place of Rest**
   Matthew 11:28–30 – "Come to Me, all who are weary…"
   If a church is breaking you instead of healing you, it's not aligned with God's will.

Reflections & Questions

1. Have I mistaken spiritual abuse for godly correction?
2. How has abuse affected my relationship with God?
3. What areas of my heart still need healing from past church wounds?
4. Have I allowed bitterness to grow because of past hurts?
5. What steps can I take toward trusting again?

Breaking the Cycle of Spiritual Abuse

1. **Acknowledge the Wound**
   Healing begins when you stop pretending you're fine. Denial keeps you stuck, but honesty brings freedom.
2. **Separate God from People**
   Many who experience abuse in church struggle to trust God, mistaking human failure for divine failure. God is your healer, not your abuser.
3. **Pursue Healing, Not Isolation**
   It's tempting to leave church altogether, but isolation doesn't heal. Seek a safe, healthy environment to rebuild trust.
4. **Allow God to Restore Your Trust**
   You can trust again without being naive. Healing doesn't mean blindly following leaders—it means walking in wisdom.
5. **Let Go of Bitterness**
   Forgiveness isn't about excusing abuse; it's about freeing yourself from its control. Holding onto offense will shape your future if you let it.

Prophetic Declarations

- I break every chain of spiritual abuse in Jesus' name.
- I am not defined by my past, but by God's purpose.
- God is my healer, and He restores my soul.
- No manipulation will hold me captive any longer.
- I release bitterness and walk in freedom.
- I will trust again, with wisdom and discernment.
- My faith is rooted in God, not in man.
- I am walking into healing and wholeness.

- The wounds of my past will not limit my future.
- I am free in Jesus' name.

Breaking Free - The 3-Step Abused Challenge

If you're serious about breaking free from spiritual abuse, consider this challenge:

1. **Find a Safe Accountability Partner**
   Connect with someone trustworthy who will walk with you through healing.
2. **Make the Above Declarations for 7 Days**
   Speak healing, freedom, and restoration over yourself.
3. **Commit to 5 Months of Intentional Healing**
   Rebuild your trust in God's way, not based on human failures.

Step 1: Find a Safe Accountability Partner

Proverbs 27:17 – "As iron sharpens iron, so one person sharpens another."

Spiritual abuse isolates. It makes you question who you can trust and whether anyone truly cares. The enemy wants you alone and silent, but healing happens in safe, healthy relationships. Choose someone who is:

- Mature in faith (they know God's Word and can guide you with truth).
- Trustworthy (no gossip or betrayal).
- Compassionate but honest (able to listen without judgment but challenge you to move forward).
- Spiritually healthy (not bitter or wounded themselves; wise enough to guide you into healing).

They can help you:
- Process pain without falling into bitterness.
- Remind you your identity is in God, not in what happened to you.
- Pray with you through your journey.
- Encourage you to walk in freedom, not remain stuck in the past.

Step 2: Make the Above Declarations for 7 Days

Romans 12:2 – "Do not conform to the pattern of this world, but be transformed by the renewing of your mind."

Abuse leaves scars—emotional, mental, and spiritual. If you don't speak truth over yourself, your pain will continue to define you. Declarations rewire your mindset by:
- Reminding you that your past doesn't define you.
- Affirming that you're not abandoned—God is restoring you.
- Pushing you to trust again with wisdom and discernment.

How to Apply:
- Say them out loud every morning and night for 7 days.
- Believe each word; let them sink deep into your spirit.
- Write them down, repeat them, and adapt them to your specific struggle.

Healing is in your words—speak life, and watch God bring restoration.

Step 3: Commit to 5 Months of Intentional Healing

Luke 16:10 – "Whoever can be trusted with very little can also be trusted with much."

Time alone doesn't heal wounds—intentionality does. Many who are abused leave their church, but the hurt remains alive inside them. Over the next 5 months:

- Avoid dwelling on the past. You acknowledge the pain but won't relive it daily.
- Don't define yourself by the abuse—you're not a victim but victorious.
- Seek healing, not avoidance—running away isn't healing.
- Find a healthy church or spiritual environment—community is necessary, but the right one.
- Let God restore your ability to trust—wisely, without being naive.

How to Apply:
- Keep a journal—track your healing journey.
- Seek counsel—mentor, pastor, or Christian therapist if needed.
- Pray for discernment—ask God to show you what healthy leadership looks like.
- Take your time—healing happens layer by layer.

Healing isn't just about moving on—it's about moving forward in wholeness.

A Contract with Yourself & God

"Lord, for the next 5 months, I commit to breaking free from spiritual abuse. I will not let my past define me. I will not live in bitterness. I will allow You to heal me fully, and I will trust again—with wisdom and discernment. My future is not in the hands of people—it is in Your hands. In Jesus' Name, Amen."

Signature: _____

Date: _____

This is your healing season. No more bondage. No more fear—only freedom, wholeness, and restoration.

Closing Prayer

Father, in the name of Jesus, I surrender every wound, betrayal, and abuse that has marked my soul. I refuse to be defined by pain. Break every chain of offense, bitterness, and fear. Restore my trust in Your church. Heal my heart so I can walk in my calling without fear. Where I was broken, make me whole; where I was wounded, make me a vessel of healing. I move forward in faith, free from my past. In Jesus' mighty name, Amen.

Final Words

Are you an Abused believer? Have you allowed spiritual wounds to distance you from God and His people?
Decide today to pursue healing, trust again, and move forward in freedom. Your story isn't over—this is the beginning of your restoration.

Below is **Chapter Five: The Rejected**, with Aniyah's story inserted, followed by the profile, biblical insights, challenge sections, and closing prayer. It has been reformatted for clarity and consistency, with minor grammar and punctuation corrections, and all emojis removed.

CHAPTER FIVE: THE REJECTED

Confessions of the Rejected: The Story of Aniyah

Aniyah had experienced rejection long before she ever set foot in a church.

As the oldest of six children, she was raised in a home where love felt like a privilege, not a guarantee. While other children enjoyed bedtime stories and warm embraces, Aniyah was met with cold silences and harsh words. Her mother was too occupied with survival to offer affection, and her father was a ghost—a presence that haunted but never remained.

She grew up feeling invisible, convinced love was something to be earned. So she worked tirelessly for approval, hoping that if she did enough—if she became enough—someone, anyone, would finally see her.

Then she met Derrick: smooth, charming, and full of promises. He made her feel beautiful, special, and irreplaceable. For the first time, someone made her feel wanted. She gave him everything—her trust, her body, her heart. In return, he gave her a child.

The Ultimate Rejection

When she told him she was pregnant, she assumed he would step up. She envisioned a home, a future, and the family she never had. But Derrick had other plans. Within a year, he married another woman—a stranger in Aniyah's eyes—worthy of his commitment.

Aniyah was left behind, abandoned, raising her daughter alone. The rejection cut deep, and she vowed never to be vulnerable again. Yet pain has a way of shaping a person. In Aniyah's case, it made her reckless.

- She hated feeling unwanted, so she sought validation from men.
- She hated feeling unseen, so she became the loudest in any room.
- She hated feeling powerless, so she wielded her words like weapons—gossip, slander, manipulation—anything to stay in control.

By the time she had six children from different men, she had mastered the art of survival. She had also built a life of brokenness—never staying in one place long enough to be truly known, never trusting enough to be truly loved.

Then one day, she found the church—or rather, the church found her.

A New Beginning... Or So She Thought

A neighbor had been inviting her to church for months. "Come, Aniyah. Just try it once." She always refused, convinced church people were fake—holy on the outside, but gossiping behind your back. But one night, something inside her broke. She was exhausted—physically, emotionally, spiritually. With nothing left to lose, she went.

For the first time in her life, she felt peace. The worship touched her in ways she never thought possible. The message felt tailor-made for her. When the pastor called people to the altar, she walked forward, tears streaming down her face. That day, Aniyah gave her life to Jesus. For the first time, she felt chosen—seen—accepted. She thought she had finally found a place where she belonged.

But rejection has a way of following you.

Who Is the Rejected?

The Rejected are those who feel unseen, forgotten, or overlooked in their environment—those who assume exclusion even when it isn't the case, who push people away before they can be rejected, who struggle with correction, perceiving it as a personal attack, or who feel they must prove themselves worthy to belong.

Rejection distorts perception. Even when people accept you, the wounds of past rejection convince you they do not.

Psalm 27:10 – "Though my father and mother forsake me, the Lord will receive me."
Rejection from people does not remove your acceptance in God.

Profile of the Rejected

- Do you feel unseen or overlooked in relationships, workplaces, or church?
- Do you assume people are excluding you, even when they're not?
- Do you push people away before they have a chance to reject you?
- Have you built emotional walls that make it difficult for others to get close?
- Do you misinterpret correction as a direct assault on your character?

If you answered yes to any of these, you may be wrestling with a spirit of rejection. But there is hope.

Breaking the Cycle of Rejection

1. **Recognize the Lies**
   The enemy deceives you into believing you're unloved or unwanted. Reject those lies by declaring God's Word over yourself.
2. **Heal from Past Wounds**
   Bring your pain to God. Let Him heal your heart so rejection no longer dictates your future.
3. **Surround Yourself with the Right People**
   Isolation inflames feelings of rejection. Stay connected to a supportive faith community.
4. **Renew Your Identity in Christ**
   Your value is not found in human approval—it is rooted in Christ's acceptance of you.
5. **Forgive and Move Forward**
   Holding onto past rejection keeps you trapped in the past. Forgiveness is about your freedom, not excusing others.

Prophetic Declarations

- I am chosen by God, not rejected by man.
- I break every lie of rejection in Jesus' name.
- I am fully loved and accepted in Christ.
- I will not allow past rejection to shape my future.
- I embrace correction as growth, not rejection.
- I forgive those who have rejected me.
- I belong in God's family—I do not have to prove my worth.
- My wounds are healing, and my heart is whole.

- I will not push people away in fear of rejection.
- God's love is enough for me.

The 3-Step Rejection Challenge

If you're serious about breaking free from rejection, consider this challenge:
1. **Find a Safe Accountability Partner** – Confide in someone who will support you through healing.
2. **Make the Above Declarations for 7 Days** – Speak acceptance and truth over yourself daily.
3. **Commit to 5 Months of Intentional Relationship Building** – Stop pushing people away and learn to embrace healthy connections.

Step 1: Find a Safe Accountability Partner

The Power of Accountability in Healing Rejection

Rejection creates a cycle of isolation. It tells you you're better off alone, that no one truly cares, that people will only hurt you if you let them in. This is a lie from the enemy meant to keep you from experiencing genuine love and belonging.

One of the most critical steps in healing from rejection is **choosing to trust someone enough to walk with you** through it. You need a **safe accountability partner** who will:

- Listen without judgment.
- Help you recognize when rejection is distorting your perception.
- Encourage you to stay connected instead of withdrawing.
- Remind you of your worth when rejection tries to convince you otherwise.

They should be spiritually mature, trustworthy, compassionate yet honest, and committed to your healing.

How to Apply This Step

- **Pray** for discernment; ask God for the right person.
- Be **honest** about your struggle—let them in.
- Allow them to **challenge** your negative perceptions.
- Stay **consistent**—check in with them regularly as you walk through this journey.

Healing starts with connection. Don't run—let God place the right people around you.

Step 2: Make the Above Declarations for 7 Days

Rejection loses its power when truth becomes your foundation.

Why Declarations Matter

Rejection builds strongholds in the mind and convinces you that you're unloved, unwanted, unseen. These thoughts form your reality—until you **replace them with truth**.

Declarations serve as **weapons** against the lies of rejection. As you **speak truth** over yourself, your heart and mind start aligning with God's viewpoint instead of your past wounds.

For the next seven days:

- **Reject** the lies of rejection.
- **Affirm** your identity in Christ.
- **Declare** acceptance over your life.

How to Apply This Step

- Speak the listed declarations each morning and night for 7 days.
- Say them **aloud**—your spirit must hear them.
- Write them down and **meditate** on them throughout the day.
- When feelings of rejection arise, **combat them** with your declarations.

You are not rejected—you are chosen, loved, and accepted. Declare it until you believe it.

Step 3: Commit to 5 Months of Intentional Relationship Building

"Rejection makes you build walls, but healing teaches you to build bridges." – Joshua Selman

"If you keep pushing people away, you will never experience the love you crave." – Myles Munroe

The Power of Intentional Relationships

Rejection often leads to self-sabotage. Instead of waiting to be rejected, you push people away first, constructing walls to protect yourself. But those walls **keep love out**.

For the next **5 months**, you must commit to:

- Not withdrawing when people try to love you.
- Not assuming rejection before it happens.
- Staying in relationships even when it feels uncomfortable.
- Allowing people to show you that you are valued and loved.

Healing from rejection does not guarantee everyone will accept you; it does mean you stop letting your past define your future connections.

Why 5 Months of Intentional Relationship Building?

1. **It takes time** to rewire how you see yourself—you need consistent connection.
2. It forces you to **stop running**—healing comes when you stay.
3. It teaches you to **receive love**—the longer you practice vulnerability, the more natural it becomes.
4. It **allows community** to be a part of your healing—God never intended you to do life alone.

How to Apply This Step

- Engage in church, friendships, and community without pulling back.
- When you feel like withdrawing, fight to stay present.
- Allow people to love you instead of assuming rejection.
- Track your progress—document moments when you chose connection over isolation.

For five months, commit to staying present. Stop running. Let healing happen in relationships.

A Contract with Yourself & God

This is more than a challenge—it's a covenant between **you and God**. If you accept, sign below:

"Lord, for the next 5 months, I commit to breaking free from rejection. I will not allow past wounds to shape my future. I will trust, connect, and remain present in the relationships You have placed in my life. I am not rejected—I am chosen, loved, and accepted. In Jesus' Name, Amen."

Signature: _____

Date: _____

This is your season of acceptance. No more walls, no more isolation—only healing, connection, and freedom.

Closing Prayer

Father, in the name of Jesus, I surrender every wound, every rejection, every scar that has shaped my identity. I refuse to believe the lie that I am unloved, unseen, or unworthy. You have chosen me, You have called me, You have accepted me. I forgive those who have rejected me and release the pain. I break every lie that says I am not enough. From today forward, I will walk in the confidence of Your love. I am accepted. I am loved. I am whole. In Jesus' name, Amen.

Final Words

Rejection is one of the deepest wounds a person can carry. It shapes how you see yourself, how you relate to others, and even how you relate to God. But rejection from man does not equate to rejection from God.

Isaiah 41:9 – "I have chosen you and have not rejected you."

If people walked away, God stayed.
If they overlooked you, God called you.
If they deemed you unworthy, God sent His Son to die for you.

You are not forgotten. You are not unwanted. You are deeply loved.

This is your choice: Will you let past rejection define your present, or will you embrace Christ's acceptance?

Your story isn't over—this is the beginning of your restoration.

CHAPTER SIX: THE BLEEDING LEADER

Confessions of the Bleeding Leader: The Story of Jabari

From the moment Jabari stepped into ministry, he carried something different. In the early days—when their church could barely fill a rented storefront—he preached with a passion that lit up every corner of the room. Congregants marveled at how his charisma seemed both God-given and finely honed, as though he had been shaped for this calling long before he ever held a microphone.

He was warm, approachable, and genuinely interested in people's struggles, often spending hours in prayer, counseling, and fasting on their behalf.

In time, God rewarded that dedication: the once-tiny church exploded in membership. What started as a handful in folding chairs became a thriving congregation filling hundreds of seats. As the ministry's reputation grew, leaders from other churches came to observe his methods, eager to learn how a young pastor was leading such remarkable revival in a short span.

There were invitations to speak at conferences, offers to mentor younger ministers, and even calls from abroad asking him to share his insights. To the outside world, Jabari had it all—a booming ministry, the respect of peers, and a promising future.

But behind the scenes, his world was crumbling.

The Breaking of a Marriage

Jabari wasn't just a pastor—he was also a husband. He and Latifah met long before the crowds ever knew his name. She saw him as a passionate Bible study leader in college, brimming with dreams of one day pastoring a church to reach the lost. From day one, Latifah was his rock: supportive, loving, and just as committed to the vision God placed on his life as he was.

In the early years of their marriage, they were inseparable—the dynamic duo of ministry. She believed in his calling, and he cherished her unwavering faith in him. Yet, as the church expanded, so did the demands on Jabari's time.

Latifah tried to be understanding:
- "We're building the kingdom."
- "God is using him mightily."
- "This is our joint calling."

But as the church shifted from dozens of members to hundreds, she saw less and less of the man she married. Date nights turned into last-minute cancellations. Family dinners were replaced by late-night strategy meetings. Sleep became a luxury, and when Jabari did sleep, it was often alone in his office, poring over Scripture, sermon notes, and church growth plans.

At first, Latifah masked her pain with enthusiasm. She greeted new members, organized women's fellowships, and tried to keep the home fires burning. In private, though, she felt a growing emptiness.

One evening, after he rushed through dinner to attend yet another emergency meeting, Latifah looked him in the eyes and said, "I don't think I can do this anymore."

He froze, feeling a knot tighten in his chest. Fear gripped him—he was losing his wife. But instead of moving him toward repentance or self-examination, that fear drove him deeper into ministry. Fixing the church was easier than facing the heartbreak at home.

Who Is the Bleeding Leader?

A Bleeding Leader is someone who carries the wounds of leadership while continuing to serve others. They may be pastors, ministry leaders, or spiritual mentors who:

- Pour into others but have no one pouring into them.
- Suffer in silence, fearing that admitting weakness would disqualify them from leading.
- Continue functioning in ministry while emotionally, spiritually, or physically drained.

A Bleeding Leader doesn't recognize their own exhaustion until it's too late. They convince themselves that ministry inevitably involves suffering, that burnout, pain, and loss are part of the calling.

Matthew 11:28 – "Come to me, all you who are weary and burdened, and I will give you rest."
Ministry should be joyful service, not a life of quiet suffering.

Profile of the Bleeding Leader

- Do you find yourself pouring into others without taking time to replenish yourself?
- Do you carry silent burdens because you feel you can't afford to show weakness?
- Have you convinced yourself that pain and exhaustion are just part of ministry?

- Do you feel disconnected from God even while leading others closer to Him?
- Have you experienced isolation, depression, or deep discouragement in leadership?
- Are you more committed to keeping the ministry running than keeping your own soul healthy?

If you answered yes to several of these, you may be a Bleeding Leader.

Root Causes & Biblical Insights

1. **Leadership Without Rest Is Destructive**
   Exodus 18:18 – "You and these people who come to you will only wear yourselves out…"
   Even Moses needed rest; even Jesus withdrew to pray. Ministry shouldn't be sustained by exhaustion.

2. **Isolation Is a Trap for Leaders**
   Ecclesiastes 4:9–10 – "Two are better than one… If either falls, one can help the other up."
   Leading alone sets you up for spiritual collapse.

3. **Your First Ministry Is Your Home**
   1 Timothy 3:5 – "If anyone does not know how to manage his own family, how can he take care of God's church?"
   Neglecting family for ministry isn't sacrifice; it's being out of order.

4. **God Wants You to Be Whole, Not Just Effective**
   3 John 1:2 – "I pray that you may prosper… as your soul prospers."
   God cares about spiritual success and emotional and physical well-being.

5. **A Burnt-Out Leader Cannot Carry the Vision**
   Galatians 6:9 – "Let us not grow weary in doing good…"

Exhaustion leads to discouragement, and discouragement leads to disillusionment. Without rest, a leader eventually breaks.

Reflections & Questions

1. Have I confused suffering with sacrifice in leadership?
2. Am I caring for my spiritual health or only focusing on others?
3. Have I neglected personal relationships to build ministry?
4. Am I serving out of love or merely pushing forward from obligation?
5. What practical steps can I take to avoid burnout?

Breaking the Cycle of a Bleeding Leader

1. **Acknowledge the Wounds**
   Healing begins with admitting you are not okay. There is no shame in struggling.
2. **Prioritize Rest and Renewal**
   If Jesus withdrew to rest, you must too. Ministry flows best from rest, not perpetual exhaustion.
3. **Surround Yourself with a Support System**
   Find mentors, friends, or even a counselor who can pour into you as you pour into others.
4. **Set Healthy Boundaries**
   Learn to say no. You can't save the world at the expense of your own soul.
5. **Return to Your First Love**
   Ministry is about serving God, not just maintaining a church. Spend time in worship, personal prayer, and intimacy with Christ.

Prophetic Declarations

1. I release every silent burden I've been carrying alone.
2. I will no longer serve from a place of exhaustion but from a place of overflow.
3. God is restoring my joy in leadership.
4. I am not defined by my title, but by my relationship with Christ.
5. I will not sacrifice my well-being for the sake of ministry.
6. I embrace rest as a holy discipline.
7. I will surround myself with godly support and wisdom.
8. My family is not my sacrifice—my family is my first ministry.
9. I reject the lie that suffering in silence makes me a better leader.
10. God is refueling me, refreshing me, and giving me new strength for the journey.

The 3-Part Bleeding Leader Challenge

If you're determined to break free from burnout and lead from wholeness, consider this challenge:

1. **Find a Trusted Mentor or Friend**
   Connect with someone who can support you on your journey to healing.
2. **Make the Above Declarations for 7 Days**
   Speak healing, strength, and renewal over yourself daily.
3. **Commit to 5 Months of Intentional Self-Care and Renewal**
   For the next five months, set aside two days each week for restoration—time to focus on yourself, your family, and your time with God.

Step 1: Find a Trusted Mentor or Friend

Proverbs 11:14 – "Where there is no guidance, a people falls, but in an abundance of counselors there is safety."

Many leaders struggle alone because they believe no one understands their burden. This is a lie from the enemy—God never intended you to lead in isolation.

- **Seek wise counsel** from those who grasp both leadership and personal well-being.
- **Be transparent**—share your hardships.
- **Allow others** to pour into you as you pour into others.

Step 2: Make the Above Declarations for 7 Days

Romans 12:2 – "Be transformed by the renewing of your mind…"

Your thoughts shape your leadership. If you keep believing "this is just how ministry is," you'll remain stuck in an unhealthy cycle.

- **Speak these declarations daily**.
- **Reject false beliefs** about leadership.
- **Replace exhaustion with expectation**—God wants you restored.

Step 3: Commit to 5 Months of Intentional Self-Care and Renewal

Mark 6:31 – "Come with me by yourselves to a quiet place and get some rest."

Rest is not weakness—it's wisdom. Even Jesus pulled away from crowds for renewal.

For five months:

- **No overworking** to the point of exhaustion.
- **No ignoring personal struggles** for the sake of ministry.
- **Prioritize two days a week** for personal renewal: rest, reconnection with God, and time with family.
- **Be intentional**—spend that time reading, worshiping, reflecting, and physically resting.
- **Rebuild** areas you've neglected: your family, friendships, personal health.

Rest isn't quitting—it's preparing for greater.

A Contract with Yourself & God

This is more than a challenge—it's a covenant between you and God. If you accept, sign below:

"Lord, for the next 5 months, I commit to breaking free from leading while bleeding. I refuse to sacrifice my personal well-being or my family on the altar of ministry. I will not allow burnout, isolation, or unrealistic expectations to dictate my leadership. I will seek wisdom, accountability, and divine rest. I embrace healing, balance, and a renewed sense of purpose. I am not just a leader—I am Your child first. In Jesus' Name, Amen." If you accept, sign below as a declaration of faithfulness:

Signature: _____

Date: _____

You are more than a title—you are God's son or daughter first. Rest is not quitting; it is preparation for greater. May this covenant guide you to balanced leadership and spiritual renewal in every season.

Closing Prayer

Father, I surrender every weight, every silent burden, and every unspoken struggle I've carried in leadership. I refuse to lead while bleeding. I ask for Your healing, restoration, and strength. Renew my passion, but not at the cost of my well-being. Teach me to rest, trust, and serve from a place of wholeness. In Jesus' name, Amen.

Final Words

Leadership isn't a call to self-destruction; it's a call to serve with strength. Isaiah 40:31 – "Those who wait on the Lord will renew their strength."

You are not alone, nor forgotten, and you don't have to break under the weight of ministry. Rest is not quitting—it is preparing for greater.

CHAPTER SEVEN: THE CONFUSED

The Voices That Whispered: The Story of Layla

Layla had been part of the church for years. She wasn't just a member—she was family. She had poured her time, her heart, and her finances into the ministry. She had felt God's power there and had grown in her faith there.

But now, she stood outside the church doors, about to leave it all behind. Her mind was tormented. Her heart was heavy. She could barely recognize herself anymore.

How did she get here?
It didn't happen overnight. It started with a whisper.

A Place That Felt Safe

Layla was drawn to deep spiritual conversations. She didn't want shallow Christianity—she wanted to truly know God and His Word. So when Diane, an older church member, invited her to join a small discussion group, Layla eagerly agreed.

"We're not like the others," Diane had said with a knowing smile. "We don't just follow blindly. We ask the hard questions."

At first, these meetings were refreshing—prayer gatherings where they studied Scripture and had meaningful discussions. But over time, the atmosphere changed. Instead of focusing on God, the conversations shifted toward suspicion.

The First Seed of Doubt

One evening, they gathered in Diane's living room, the scent of cinnamon tea in the air. Mike, a sharp, business-minded man, broke the silence:

"You ever wonder why the pastor talks about money so much? Where does all that offering really go?"

Layla hesitated, defending the church at first. But then Zora chimed in with a story about someone who needed rent money and was told to "keep trusting God," while the pastor supposedly bought a new car. Levi, usually silent, suggested the church might be operating under "something else—something darker."

Their words planted a cold, unsettling doubt in Layla's heart. She had never questioned her church's sincerity before. Now, she couldn't stop.

Who Is the Confused?

The Confused are believers who:
- Have become disoriented in their faith due to conflicting voices.
- Have allowed questions to morph into suspicion instead of leading to revelation.
- Are caught between truth and deception without clarity.
- Have lost confidence in spiritual leadership and church integrity because of external influences.

James 1:6 – "The one who doubts is like a wave of the sea, blown and tossed by the wind."
Confusion is not from God—it is a tool of the enemy to destabilize your faith.

Profile of the Confused

- Do you find yourself questioning everything you once believed?
- Have you allowed negative voices to shape your perception of church and leadership?
- Do you struggle with distrust, fear, or hesitation when engaging with faith-based communities?
- Do you feel spiritually disconnected or hesitant about your church involvement?

If you answered yes to several of these, you may be wrestling with spiritual confusion.

Root Causes & Biblical Insights

1. Confusion Is a Strategy of the Enemy

1 Corinthians 14:33 – "For God is not the author of confusion, but of peace."
God brings clarity, but the enemy thrives in deception.

2. Gossip and Slander Open Doors to Doubt

Proverbs 16:28 – "A perverse person stirs up conflict, and a gossip separates close friends."
Suspicion often begins with whispered conversations, not direct offenses.

3. Be Careful Who You Let Speak Into Your Life

2 Timothy 4:3–4 – "For the time will come when people will not put up with sound doctrine... instead, they will gather around them teachers who

say what their itching ears want to hear."
Not every voice that questions is wise—some are simply divisive.

4. Isolation Magnifies Confusion

Hebrews 10:25 – "Do not give up meeting together..."
Faith grows in community; confusion grows in isolation.

Reflections & Questions

1. Have I allowed negative conversations to change my view of my church or leaders?
2. Am I seeking truth, or simply looking for reasons to validate my doubts?
3. Do I feel distant from God because of the voices I've let influence me?
4. What steps can I take to separate truth from deception?
5. How can I refocus on God rather than the opinions of others?

Breaking the Cycle of Confusion

1. **Seek God, Not Just Answers**
   While questions matter, your priority should be a closer relationship with the Lord. Intimacy with God often resolves doubts intellect alone cannot.
2. **Find Wise Counsel**
   Isolation fuels confusion. Surround yourself with mature believers, pastors, or mentors who can provide biblical perspectives and help process doubts.

3. **Anchor Yourself in the Word**
   Study Scripture diligently. Be mindful about whose teachings you follow, verifying everything against God's Word.
4. **Reject Every Whisper of Division**
   The enemy sows doubt and division through subtle whispers. Recognize when legitimate questions turn into spiritual isolation.
5. **Commit to Spiritual Clarity**
   Choose to seek wisdom from God's Word rather than be swayed by human opinions.

Prophetic Declarations

- I reject every lie and spirit of confusion in Jesus' name.
- My faith is rooted in God, not in the whispers of doubt.
- I receive clarity and wisdom to discern truth from deception.
- I will not allow gossip or slander to shape my perception of God's house.
- I walk in divine understanding, free from spiritual confusion.
- My mind is renewed daily by the Word of God.
- I submit my questions to God and trust His timing.
- I will not let my faith be shaken by the opinions of others.
- God is leading me into truth, step by step.
- I am anchored in Christ, unshaken by confusion.

The 3-Step Confusion Challenge

If you're serious about breaking free from confusion, take this challenge:

1. **Talk to Your Pastor** – Seek guidance from the leader God has placed over your life.

2. **Make the Above Declarations for 7 Days** – Speak clarity and spiritual discernment over yourself daily.
3. **Commit to 5 Months of Anchoring in the Word** – Distance yourself from unordained relationships, silence unqualified voices, and stay submitted to the spiritual leaders God has placed over you.

Step 1: Talk to Your Pastor

The Power of Seeking Spiritual Covering

Confusion often arises when people disconnect from spiritual leadership and try to handle their faith alone. If you find yourself struggling with doubts, conflicting voices, or mistrust toward church leadership, a good place to start is **seeking clarity from your pastor**—the person God has placed in your life for spiritual guidance.

- They will help you separate truth from deception.
- They will guide you in finding a godly accountability partner.
- They will help realign you with biblical truth when emotions lead you astray.
- They will cover you in prayer and offer wisdom for your spiritual journey.

How to Apply This Step:

- Schedule a conversation with your pastor to discuss your spiritual struggles.
- Be honest about your confusion, doubts, or negative influences.
- Receive their counsel with an open and teachable heart.
- Ask them to help you find a mature accountability partner who will walk with you.

Your freedom from confusion starts with aligning under God's established order.

Step 2: Make the Above Declarations for 7 Days

Why Declarations Matter

Confusion is a spiritual attack designed to weaken your faith. The enemy thrives on deception, using subtle whispers to make you question what you once believed. Truth is a weapon—speaking God's Word over yourself helps break confusion.

For seven days:

- Declare clarity over your mind.
- Reject confusion and deception.
- Align your words with Scripture.

How to Apply This Step:

- Speak these declarations aloud morning and night for seven days.
- Say them with faith—your spirit must hear them.
- Write them down and meditate on them throughout the day.
- When confusion arises, respond with declarations of truth.

Confusion loses its hold when you declare God's truth over your life.

Step 3: Commit to 5 Months of Anchoring in the Word

The Power of Staying Anchored

Confusion grows where truth is absent. Many struggle because they rely on opinions, emotions, or one-off experiences rather than daily engagement with the Word of God. Lasting clarity comes by committing to a season of being anchored in God's truth.

For five months:

- Remove yourself from relationships and conversations that God did not ordain.
- Distance yourself from gossip, slander, and negative speech.
- Stop seeking advice from those who are not spiritually positioned to give it.
- Stop feeding your doubts with social media debates and conflicting doctrines.

Why 5 Months?

1. **The Word brings clarity**—as you read it daily, deception loses its grip.
2. **You recognize false voices**—when you know what's real, counterfeits become obvious.
3. **Faith grows through consistent study**—confusion fades as truth becomes your foundation.
4. **Spiritual maturity requires stability**—jumping between opinions weakens your faith; being anchored in God strengthens it.
5. **Relationships shape your faith**—if you surround yourself with confusion, you will remain confused. If you surround yourself with truth, you will be established.

How to Apply This Step:

- Remove yourself from unproductive groups or friendships that foster doubt.
- Guard your ears—reject gossip or slander about your leaders or church.
- Stop listening to multiple teachers—remain under the covering God has assigned you.

- Revisit sermons from your church instead of seeking new teachings online.
- Make Scripture your primary source of wisdom—seek God's voice above all.

For five months, commit to staying planted. No more mixed voices, no more confusion—only spiritual clarity and stability.

A Contract with Yourself & God

This is more than a challenge—it's a covenant between you and God. If you accept, sign below:

"Lord, for the next 5 months, I commit to breaking free from confusion. I will not allow deception to rule my faith. I will seek wisdom, stay anchored in Your Word, and submit to the spiritual leaders You have placed over me. I will remove myself from negative conversations, unordained relationships, and voices that breed division. I refuse to chase multiple teachings; I will remain planted in the truth You have given me. My faith is rooted in You alone. In Jesus' Name, Amen."

Signature: _____

Date: _____

This is your season of clarity. No more deception, no more doubt—only wisdom, truth, and spiritual confidence.

Closing Prayer

Father, in the mighty name of Jesus, I come before You with every doubt, every unanswered question, and every uncertainty that has clouded my heart. I choose to trust You above all else.

Break every spirit of deception that seeks to lead me astray. Open my eyes to Your truth and surround me with wise, godly counsel. I declare that confusion will not uproot my faith or separate me from Your presence.

Holy Spirit, guide me into all truth as I anchor myself in Your Word. In Jesus' name, **Amen.**

CHAPTER EIGHT: THE INDEPENDENT SPIRIT

Confessions of the Independent Spirit: The Story of Zahir

Zahir was not an ordinary church member. He was brilliant, well-educated, and deeply spiritual. From a young age, he had a hunger for knowledge, excelling in everything he tried. He questioned everything—not out of rebellion, but because he believed he was meant to operate at a higher level of understanding.

To him, submission was for those who didn't know any better:
- "God speaks to me directly—I don't need a mediator."
- "Why should I submit to people who know less than me?"
- "Titles don't mean anything. We're all equal before God."

Zahir wasn't anti-church—he simply believed no one was qualified to lead him.

The Rise of an Untouchable Mind

Zahir's wisdom was his greatest gift—and also his greatest downfall. He had a profound understanding of Scripture, and his insights fascinated people. However, this knowledge bred a quiet arrogance. He saw himself as "above" traditional church structures.

He often said:
- "Submission to church leadership is optional. God is my covering."

- "I have deeper revelation; they can't teach me anything new."

Signs of the Independent Spirit

At first, these signs seemed harmless, even admirable. But they revealed a deeper issue:

- In Bible studies, he always raised his hand—not to learn, but to share his "higher" revelation.
- He refused to join group outings, choosing instead to remain separate and self-sufficient.
- During corporate fasts, he would do his own fast or claim God told him not to fast.
- Sometimes he skipped Sunday services altogether, citing personal study or "a leading from the Spirit."
- He refused to address the pastor by any title, insisting, "We're all just brothers in Christ."
- When corrected, he became defensive, calling the rebuke "carnal correction."

In Zahir's mind, he was not rebellious—he was simply "free."

Building a Ministry Within a Ministry

It started small. After services, Zahir began hosting informal discussion groups where people could "go deeper" into topics the pastor had preached. Initially, just a few curious members attended. Over time, these gatherings grew into their own separate movement.

- People started attending his group instead of the church's official Bible studies.
- His teachings became increasingly critical of leadership, suggesting they were "limiting revelation."

- He emphasized that no one needed a covering because the Holy Spirit led them all.

Eventually, the pastor confronted him:

"Zahir, I love you, but you are building a ministry inside a ministry. That is out of order."

Zahir crossed his arms.

"I'm just teaching people the truth."

"Under whose authority?" the pastor asked. "You are not submitted to this house."

"I don't need to be," Zahir replied. "God is my covering."

The meeting ended with Zahir leaving the church. Days later, he launched his own ministry.

A Ministry Without Authority

Zahir's ministry thrived at first:
- His livestreams drew thousands of viewers.
- He was popular, respected, and in demand.
- His messages were bold, controversial, and challenging.

But something was missing: **true spiritual authority.** His knowledge could persuade minds, but it lacked the anointing to transform hearts.

The Night of the Manifestation

A turning point came during one of his major conferences. The event was packed, the atmosphere electric. As he preached, a woman in the audience suddenly screamed and fell to the floor, convulsing violently—demonically manifesting.

Zahir stepped forward to cast it out:

"I command you to leave in Jesus' name!"

Nothing happened. The demon laughed:

"You have no authority over me. I know the ministry you came from… I know your pastor… but you? You are not known."

Zahir's blood ran cold. He shouted prayers, but the demon didn't move. Instead, the possessed woman struck him, knocking him back. Ushers rushed to help, and Zahir stood there, shaken. He remembered watching his old pastor cast out demons effortlessly, carrying true authority. Zahir had taken knowledge but **rejected submission**, and now he was powerless against a real spiritual challenge.

The Fall of an Independent Man

After that night, everything crumbled:

- Attendance and excitement around his ministry faded.
- His marriage suffered; his wife saw his struggles but couldn't reach him.
- Even his business faced unexpected setbacks.

Broken and alone, he heard a whisper in his spirit:

"Go back."

He knew it meant returning to the pastor he'd dismissed. Tears filled his eyes as he dialed his old pastor's number.

"Pastor… I need help."

A pause—then a warm, fatherly voice:

"Come home, son."

That Sunday, Zahir walked into the church he once viewed with disdain. His pastor reached out and prayed over him. **In that moment, Zahir finally received what he had rejected for so long: covering, submission, and restoration.** He returned not as a leader, but as a **son**.

Who Is the Independent Spirit?

The **Independent Spirit** is the believer who rejects accountability, structure, and community. They want the **benefits of God without the design of God.** They:

- Believe they don't need a covering.
- Resist correction or leadership.
- Value personal revelations over biblical accountability.
- Slowly isolate themselves without realizing it.

Proverbs 18:1 – "A man who isolates himself seeks his own desire; he rages against all wise judgment."

Independence in the kingdom often disguises itself as wisdom, but it is frequently spiritual rebellion instead.

Profile of the Independent Spirit

- Do you struggle with submitting to spiritual authority?
- Have you convinced yourself you don't need a pastor, mentor, or covering?
- Do you resist correction, seeing it as unnecessary?

- Do you prefer to operate outside church structure rather than within it?
- Have you distanced yourself from spiritual community, believing you are fine on your own?
- Do you value your own revelation over biblical accountability?

If you answered yes to several of these, you may be wrestling with an Independent Spirit.

Hebrews 13:17 – "Obey your leaders and submit to them, for they keep watch over your souls."

Root Causes & Biblical Insights

1. **A Rebellious Spirit Disguising Itself as Wisdom**
   1 Samuel 15:23 – "Rebellion is as sinful as witchcraft…"
   Independence can be rebellion in disguise.

2. **Isolation Leads to Deception**
   Proverbs 18:1 – "A man who isolates himself seeks his own desire…"
   Separation from godly authority often leads to spiritual blindness.

3. **Authority Is God's Design, Not Man's**
   Romans 13:1 – "There is no authority except that which God has established…"
   Rejecting authority is rejecting God's established order.

4. **Submission Is the Path to True Power**
   James 4:7 – "Submit to God. Resist the devil, and he will flee…"
   You cannot have authority unless you are under authority.

5. **Covering Is for Protection, Not Control**
   2 Kings 2:9 – "Let me inherit a double portion of your spirit," Elisha said to Elijah.

Elisha received power because he honored covering. Independence blocks impartation.

Reflections & Questions

1. Have I rejected submission, seeing it as unnecessary?
2. Do I struggle with correction, always believing I'm right?
3. Am I operating in isolation, thinking I don't need spiritual family?
4. Have I convinced myself I'm the only one with the "true revelation"?
5. What steps can I take to resubmit to godly leadership?

Breaking the Cycle of an Independent Spirit

1. **Recognize That You Need Covering**
   Even Jesus submitted to the Father. If Christ needed authority, so do you.
2. **Reconnect With Spiritual Community**
   Independence leads to deception. Surround yourself with godly leaders.
3. **Humble Yourself to Correction**
   Accept godly rebuke and instruction as gifts.
4. **Realign With God's Order**
   Kingdom authority is structured. You cannot bypass biblical leadership.
5. **Commit to Serving Under Leadership**
   Elisha served Elijah before receiving the mantle. Submission precedes promotion.

Prophetic Declarations

- I break free from every independent spirit in Jesus' name.
- I submit to godly leadership and covering.
- I reject rebellion and embrace humility.
- I will not isolate myself—I choose godly community.
- I value correction because it brings wisdom.
- I will not seek power without submission.
- I will not elevate my own revelation above biblical order.
- I am covered, protected, and walking in spiritual alignment.
- I submit to God's order, and I walk in divine authority.
- God's covering over my life is my place of safety.

The 3-Step Independence Challenge

If you want to break free from an Independent Spirit, consider this challenge:

1. **Talk to Your Pastor or Mentor** – Seek alignment under godly authority.
2. **Make the Above Declarations for 7 Days** – Speak humility, submission, and covering over your life daily.
3. **Commit to 5 Months of Serving Under Leadership** – Actively submit to a mentor, pastor, or ministry leader and follow their guidance.

Step 1: Talk to Your Pastor or Mentor

The Power of Spiritual Covering

Independence convinces you that you don't need anyone, but **God designed spiritual authority to protect and grow you**. Without it, you are vulnerable to deception, spiritual pride, and stagnation.

Proverbs 11:14 – "Where there is no guidance, a people falls, but in an abundance of counselors there is safety."

How to Apply This Step:

- Seek wise counsel from a pastor or mentor who cares about your growth.
- Be transparent about your struggle with independence.
- Ask for accountability—allow them to challenge your mindset.
- Stay consistent and connected to the leadership God has placed over you.

Submission isn't bondage—it's God's ordained path to protection.

Step 2: Make the Above Declarations for 7 Days

Why Declarations Matter

The independent spirit is rooted in pride, rebellion, and rejection of correction. To break free, you must **renew your mind** and shift your heart posture toward submission.

Romans 12:2 – "Be transformed by the renewing of your mind…"

For seven days:

- Declare humility and submission over your life.
- Reject rebellion and pride in your speech.

- Replace independence with a commitment to biblical order.

Speak it until you believe it. **Submission leads to elevation** in God's Kingdom.

Step 3: Commit to 5 Months of Serving Under Leadership

The Power of Serving Under Authority

A genuine test of humility is **service**. Many want impartation without submission, promotion without process, and leadership without accountability—but that is not God's way.

Hebrews 13:17 – "Obey your leaders and submit to them, for they keep watch over your souls."

For the next five months:

- **Stay committed** to a pastor, mentor, or leader.
- **Serve** in your church or ministry with a willing heart.
- **Follow leadership's guidance** even when it's challenging.
- **Stop running** from correction or accountability.

Serving under leadership is not limitation—it is **preparation**.

A Contract with Yourself & God

This is more than a challenge—it is a covenant between **you and God**. If you accept, sign below as a declaration of faithfulness:

"Lord, for the next 5 months, I commit to breaking free from an Independent Spirit. I will not walk uncovered. I will submit to godly authority, serve under leadership, and remain accountable. I reject pride, rebellion, and isolation. I embrace humility, order, and correction. My life will be aligned with Your structure, and I will grow under the covering You have placed over me. In Jesus' Name, Amen."

Signature: _____

Date: _____

This is your season of alignment. No more rebellion. No more isolation—only growth, submission, and divine order.

Closing Prayer

Father, I repent for every time I rejected Your order. I lay down pride, rebellion, and isolation. I submit to Your design, and I receive the protection of spiritual covering. Remove every independent mindset from my heart. Teach me to walk in humility, obedience, and divine order. In Jesus' name, Amen.

CHAPTER NINE: THE OFFENDED

Coming Full Circle: The Birth of "Before You Leave"

Jabari had lost everything.

- His church had fallen apart.
- His marriage had ended.
- His faith had been shaken.

The man who had once led thousands now found himself without a pulpit, without a congregation, without a name. Yet, in the stillness of his lowest moment, God spoke:

"You are still called."

At first, he resisted. How could he lead again? He had failed. He had bled out on the battlefield of ministry, and no one had been there to stop it. But the call of God is not easily ignored.

Through months of healing, restoration, and deep inner work, Jabari found a new purpose. His greatest failure birthed his greatest calling. He built something different—not another church or platform for self-glory, but a place for the wounded. A place for those like him who had walked away, been hurt, and allowed offense to lead them out of their destiny.

He called it: **Before You Leave**.

And now, for the first time, its doors were open.

The Invitation That Brought Them Back Together

The seminar was small, held in an intimate venue designed for open dialogue and healing. The **Before You Leave** Conference was unlike any church service:

- No loud music.
- No extravagant pulpit.
- Just chairs set in a circle, a room filled with those who had left churches for various reasons, and one man who understood them all.

Jabari had sent out invitations, and each person arrived for a unique reason:

- **Sarah (The Hopper)** saw the flyer on social media. She had been to dozens of churches, none truly feeling like home.
- **Andrew (The Blamer)** received the invite from an old church member. He was skeptical but curious—maybe he wasn't alone in his church issues.
- **Naomi (The Attention Seeker)** heard about it from a former mentor. She thought she had moved on, but something about the event lingered in her mind.
- **Elijah (The Abused)** got a private message. He felt anger at first—why return to a space filled with church people? Yet something urged him to go.
- **Aniyah (The Rejected)** was told about the seminar by a coworker who knew her story. She came with no expectations, but curiosity drew her.
- **Layla (The Confused)** saw the flyer in an email chain. She had been disconnected so long, she barely remembered church life. Yet she felt something stir inside her.

- **Zahir (The Independent Spirit)** stumbled upon an ad while scrolling late at night. A seminar about staying in church? He laughed, but the idea unsettled him.

One by one, they arrived. Some recognized each other; some did not. Some had left the church at different times, but they had all come from the same place. As they entered, they were handed notebooks labeled "Before You Leave," each with a personal note from Jabari:

"This is not a place to judge, but a place to heal. You are not here by accident."

The room was filled with tension, curiosity, and unspoken wounds.

Who Is the Offended?

The **Offended** believer is someone who has allowed pain, betrayal, or unmet expectations to grow into deep resentment. Rather than seeking healing or resolution, they carry an internal offense that distorts their view of church, community, and sometimes even God Himself.

Proverbs 18:19 – "A brother offended is harder to be won than a strong city."

Offense often appears as:
- Constant distrust of leaders or fellow believers.
- An inability to hear correction without anger.
- Isolation or withdrawal from the community.
- Dwelling on past hurts instead of moving forward.

Profile of the Offended

- Do you replay certain church hurts or betrayals in your mind, feeling the same anger or sadness?
- Have you withdrawn from church involvement because you expect to be hurt again?
- Do you avoid conversations about past church experiences to keep from feeling upset?
- Do you resent people who have moved on while you still feel stuck in pain?
- Have you shut down any chance for reconciliation, convinced it wouldn't make a difference?

If you answered yes to several of these, you may be carrying an offense that needs healing.

Root Causes & Biblical Insights

1. **Offense Builds Walls That Keep Out Healing**
   Proverbs 18:19 – "A brother offended is harder to be won than a strong city."
   The longer offense remains, the harder it is to remove.

2. **Offense Is a Snare in the Last Days**
   Matthew 24:10 – "And then many will be offended…"
   Offense is one of the enemy's greatest weapons in the end times.

3. **We Cannot Avoid Offense, but We Can Choose Our Response**
   Luke 17:1 – "It is impossible that no offenses should come…"
   Being offended is inevitable; staying offended is a choice.

Reflections & Questions

1. How have I allowed offense to shape my actions or decisions?
2. Have I blamed God or others for unresolved pain?
3. What steps am I willing to take to pursue healing and restoration?
4. Do I believe genuine forgiveness is possible, even if I never receive an apology?
5. How might God use my story of offense for a greater purpose if I surrender it to Him?

Breaking the Cycle of Offense

1. **Acknowledge the Hurt**
   Pretending you're not hurt only prolongs the pain. Admit the reality so healing can begin.
2. **Choose Forgiveness**
   Forgiveness isn't a feeling; it's an act of obedience that frees you. You are not excusing the offense but refusing to let it control you.
3. **Pursue Reconciliation Where Possible**
   Some relationships can be restored, others may not—but keep your heart open to healing.
4. **Seek Healing Community**
   Isolation strengthens offense. Surround yourself with believers who encourage and challenge you to move past your pain.
5. **Let God Heal You Completely**
   Moving on isn't the same as moving forward; only God can bring complete restoration.

Prophetic Declarations

- I release every offense and embrace freedom.
- Bitterness will not poison my destiny.
- I forgive, even when it's hard.
- I will not allow past pain to dictate my future.
- My heart is healed, and my spirit is whole.
- I refuse to be a prisoner of my past.
- God is restoring my joy and peace.
- I embrace love, not resentment.
- I am walking in freedom, healing, and restoration.
- Nothing will separate me from my divine assignment.

The 3-Step Offense Challenge

If you are serious about breaking free from offense, try this challenge:

1. **Talk to Your Pastor or a Trusted Mentor**
   Seek wise counsel to help process and release your offense.
2. **Make the Above Declarations for 7 Days**
   Speak healing, forgiveness, and freedom over your life daily.
3. **Commit to 5 Months of Intentional Healing and Reconciliation**
   Pursue restoration where possible, release bitterness, and rebuild trust in godly community.

Step 1: Talk to Your Pastor or a Trusted Mentor

The Power of Processing Offense in a Safe Space

Offense festers in silence. Many people withdraw from spiritual leaders and the church when they feel hurt, letting their pain shape their perspective instead of processing it with truth and wisdom.

Proverbs 19:20 – "Listen to advice and accept discipline, and at the end you will be counted among the wise."

How to Apply This Step:

- Be honest about the hurt, but remain open to truth.
- Allow a pastor or mentor to challenge your perspective if needed.
- Resist justifying bitterness—seek real healing.
- Ask for prayer and accountability to walk through the process.

No more internalizing pain without dealing with it. No more making assumptions without communication. No more letting offense dictate your actions.

Step 2: Make the Above Declarations for 7 Days

Why Declarations Matter

Offense traps the heart and mind in a cycle of replaying pain and justifying bitterness. It convinces you that you are protecting yourself, but you're actually keeping yourself bound.

Proverbs 18:21 – "The tongue has the power of life and death."

For the next 7 days:

- Declare that you are free from offense.
- Reject bitterness and resentment.

- Speak forgiveness, even if your emotions haven't aligned yet.

No more replaying past hurts in your mind. No more speaking negatively about those who hurt you. No more letting offense steal your joy.

Your words shape your reality. Speak healing, and let your heart follow.

Step 3:
Commit to 5 Months of Intentional Healing and Reconciliation

The Power of Releasing Offense and Rebuilding Trust

Healing from offense is not about pretending nothing happened. It's about choosing to release the pain so it no longer controls you. Some relationships can be restored, others may not—but your heart must remain open to healing, forgiveness, and reconciliation wherever possible.

Colossians 3:13 – "Bear with each other and forgive one another... Forgive as the Lord forgave you."

For the next 5 months:

- Let go of bitterness, choosing forgiveness even without an apology.
- Seek reconciliation where it's possible and wise.
- Reconnect with godly community—don't isolate in offense.
- Be intentional about rebuilding trust with the people God has placed in your life.

No more avoiding difficult conversations that could lead to healing. No more assuming every church or leader will hurt you. No more allowing offense to push you away from your divine assignment.

Freedom is found in releasing offense and choosing love over bitterness.

A Contract with Yourself & God

This is more than a challenge—it is a covenant between **you and God**. If you accept this commitment, sign below as a declaration of faithfulness:

"Lord, for the next 5 months, I commit to breaking free from offense. I will not allow past pain to define my future. I will seek wisdom, embrace healing, and choose forgiveness daily. I refuse to be bound by bitterness, and I open my heart to reconciliation where possible. My destiny is too great to be hindered by offense. I walk in love, freedom, and spiritual maturity. In Jesus' Name, Amen."

Signature: _____

Date: _____

This is your season of release. No more bitterness. No more offense—only healing, reconciliation, and freedom.

Closing Prayer

Father, in the mighty name of Jesus, I lay down every offense, every unresolved hurt, and every root of bitterness before You. I refuse to let pain dictate my future. I choose forgiveness. Holy Spirit, mend every broken place in my heart. Teach me to trust again, to love again, and to believe that healing is possible. I surrender my hurt and receive Your peace. In Jesus' name, Amen.

Final Words

Offense is a heavy burden to carry, yet many choose to hold onto it rather than release it. But the truth is, you cannot walk into your future while dragging the pain of your past.

Matthew 6:14 – "For if you forgive others their trespasses, your heavenly Father will also forgive you."

Let go. Release the weight. Step into freedom.
Your destiny is too great to be hindered by offense. This is your season of breakthrough.

CHAPTER TEN: WHAT WAS THE REASON THAT YOU STARTED?

Why Are You Really Leaving?

Before you take that final step—before you walk away from what you once called a divine assignment—have you stopped to ask **why**?

Do you remember the passion, the fire, and the conviction you felt when you first told God, "Lord, I will serve You"? Do you remember the tears you shed in His presence, telling Him, "Use me, Lord, whatever the cost"? Now something has shifted. Pain, disappointment, and discouragement have dimmed the flame, and you are ready to leave.

But did God truly release you, or are you releasing yourself? Too many make permanent decisions based on temporary emotions:

- You feel ignored, so you want to leave.
- You feel unappreciated, so you want to step back.
- You feel attacked, so you want to protect yourself by quitting.

Is this really the will of God, or are you reacting in the flesh?

The Danger of Emotional Decisions

One of the enemy's greatest deceptions is to make you believe that because you feel pain, you have a right to leave. Yet **pain is not always a sign to stop**; sometimes, pain is the proof you are in the right place.

In Scripture, people often destroyed their destinies by deciding in moments of frustration:

- **Esau** lost his birthright over a bowl of stew (Genesis 25:29–34). Hunger clouded his vision. He chose immediate relief over long-term inheritance.
- **Peter** nearly walked away after denying Jesus (Luke 22:61–62). Shame made him think he was no longer worthy, but Jesus restored him.
- **The Israelites** wanted to return to Egypt (Numbers 14:3–4). They preferred bondage over the process of transition. Instead of pushing forward to the promised land, they longed for the familiar, even though it was slavery.

Many have walked away from their calling—not because God led them out, but because they could no longer endure the process. The question is not, "Do I feel like leaving?" but rather, "Am I making this decision in wisdom, or am I reacting out of emotion?"

Trials Are Part of the Process

God never promised that serving Him would be easy. He never said you wouldn't face criticism or days of wanting to quit. But He did say this:

- **James 1:2–4** – "Count it all joy... when you meet trials... the testing of your faith produces steadfastness."
- **Hebrews 12:7** – "Endure hardship as discipline; God is treating you as His children."
- **1 Peter 4:12–13** – "Do not be surprised at the fiery trial... But rejoice... you share Christ's sufferings."

If hardship was a sign to give up, **Paul** would have quit after his first beating, **Peter** would have stayed a fisherman, and **Jesus** would never have carried the cross. But trials were part of their journey. The breaking, the crushing, the waiting—it was all necessary for their next level.

So again: **Why are you leaving?**

- Are you leaving because the Lord has truly spoken, or because it hurts?
- Are you leaving because your season ended, or because offense has built a wall around your heart?
- Do you remember why you started?

The Cost of Walking Away

Before you decide, understand this: **Walking away always costs something.** It is not just about leaving a church or ministry—it is about what you forfeit spiritually.

The earth has four seasons, each with its climate and opportunities. You don't plant seeds in winter and expect a harvest. Likewise, in life, when you miss a season, there is no guarantee that same season will ever return in your lifetime.

- The Israelites missed their season by complaining and longing for Egypt (Numbers 14). They allowed offense and frustration to blind them to their moment of crossover. They delayed so severely that they missed their opportunity entirely, leaving a new generation to enter the promise.

Consider these scriptures:

- **Hebrews 10:25** – "Do not forsake the assembling of the brethren…" Leaving can mean disconnecting from spiritual accountability, covering, and fellowship.

- **2 Timothy 4:10** – "Demas has forsaken me…" Many who leave fail to realize the enemy is subtly leading them from their divine assignment.
- **John 6:66–68** – "From that time many… walked with Him no more." Some disciples left Jesus because they could not handle the weight of truth.

Walking away is easy; endurance is costly. Yet only endurance leads to glory.

What Are You Really Giving Up?

Think about all you have built with the church you're considering leaving: the time, the money, the resources, the ideas, and even your heart. Now, because of offense or a difficult season, you're willing to walk away from it all?

Would you invest years in a business—only to abandon it after one bad quarter?

Since when did God use comfort as His primary tool for spiritual growth? Often, it is the struggles and trials that produce real maturity.

Some say, "Don't let anyone take your seat at the table." You have spent years serving and planting—not just for yourself but for your children, who have witnessed your devotion. Why abandon the seat you worked so hard to secure, letting someone else reap the benefits of your labor?

Offense: The Enemy's Greatest Weapon

Offense is not just a feeling; it is a spiritual strategy to remove people from their destiny. It can be so potent that a person abandons their calling entirely.

- **Yes**, sometimes you are genuinely mistreated.
- **Yes**, sometimes you do nothing wrong.

But your reaction can turn your "right" into a "wrong." If offense is what drives you out, you have surrendered your victory to the enemy. If God placed you there, it must be God who sends you out—not pain or frustration.

Were You Sent, or Did You Just Go?

One of the most dangerous things is to walk away from a place God assigned you to—**without His instruction.** It's not simply, "Am I leaving?" but "Am I being sent?" Because if God didn't send you, then you just went.

Many people claim they're led by the Spirit when, in reality, they're led by pain, frustration, or impatience. Leaving without being sent places you outside God's will, exposing you to warfare and isolation.

- **Acts 13:2** – "The Holy Spirit said, 'Set apart for Me Barnabas and Saul…'" (They were sent, not self-appointed.)
- **1 John 2:19** – "They went out from us, but they were not of us…" (Some leave, not because God called them, but because they were never truly planted.)
- **Ruth 1:16** – "Where you go, I will go…" (Ruth understood divine connection and refused to leave Naomi.)

Moving without God can birth unnecessary storms. **Jonah** ran from God's assignment and ended in the belly of a fish (Jonah 1:1–3). Leaving prematurely can bring dryness, confusion, or the loss of spiritual covering.

Spiritual Covering Is Protection, Not Control

Many reject spiritual covering as if it's control, but consider a roof: it doesn't exist to control you; it protects you from the rain. Similarly, God's system of covering protects you from spiritual harm.

- **Hebrews 13:17** – "Obey your leaders and submit to them, for they keep watch over your souls."
- **Matthew 8:9** – "For I myself am a man under authority…" (Authority is given to those who stay under it.)
- **Psalm 133:2–3** – The anointing flows from the head down. Removing yourself from divine order means removing yourself from the flow of blessing.

Faithfulness & Endurance - The Mark of True Believers

In every generation, some start well but fail to finish. Many begin with passion and conviction, but when hardship comes, they walk away. **Endurance is the mark of those who truly belong to God.**

- **Matthew 24:13** – "He who endures to the end shall be saved."
- **1 Corinthians 4:2** – "It is required of stewards to be found faithful."
- **Hebrews 6:12** – "Do not become sluggish, but imitate those who through faith and patience inherit the promises."

Growth is never comfortable. Just as a child feels growing pains, so does a believer in the process of maturing. Too many people measure their walk with God by their emotions. They assume discomfort means something is wrong—but often, discomfort is a sign of growth.

God Rewards Those Who Stay the Course

The Bible is full of men and women who **chose endurance over convenience**:

- **Joseph** endured prison but was elevated to the palace (Genesis 41:39–41).
- **David** fled Saul's attacks yet eventually sat on the throne (2 Samuel 5:3–4).
- **Paul** suffered beatings, shipwrecks, and imprisonments but finished his race (2 Timothy 4:7).

Their common thread? **They remained faithful.** God does not promote quitters. In a generation seeking instant gratification, the kingdom's currency is faithfulness.

- **Luke 16:10** – "He who is faithful in what is least is also faithful in much."
- **Galatians 6:9** – "Let us not grow weary while doing good… for in due season we shall reap if we do not lose heart."

Endurance is the doorway to destiny. Many walk away, never realizing their breakthrough was just around the corner.

Faithfulness in Seasons of Silence

Another great test is serving in a place where it seems like **nothing is changing**:

- **Moses** spent 40 years in the wilderness before stepping into leadership.
- **Abraham** waited 25 years for Isaac.
- **Jesus** spent 30 years in obscurity before His public ministry.

What if they had walked away? Some of the greatest transformations occur in hidden or silent seasons. God sees your labor, even when people don't (Hebrews 6:10). If you stay faithful, He will reward you openly (Matthew 6:4).

Reflection & Self-Examination

1. Have you truly sought God in prayer and fasting, or have you already made up your mind to leave?
2. Are you leaving because of hardship, or is God genuinely leading you elsewhere?
3. Have you discussed your decision with mature spiritual leaders, or are you isolating yourself?
4. Are you prioritizing comfort over spiritual growth?
5. Have you considered the long-term cost of walking away—from both your calling and your spiritual inheritance?

Some decisions cannot be undone. Some seasons do not return. **Do not make a choice today that costs you your destiny tomorrow.**

A Call to Remember Why You Started

God is not looking for those who merely **start** well. He wants those who **finish** well.

- **2 Timothy 4:7** – "I have fought the good fight, I have finished the race, I have kept the faith."
- **Hebrews 12:1** – "Let us run with endurance the race that is set before us."
- **Revelation 3:11** – "Hold fast what you have, that no one may take your crown."

There will always be trials and moments you feel like giving up. Yet the real question is: **Do you trust God enough to endure?**

- Some of you need to remember the passion that first led you to serve God.
- Some of you need to repent for a hasty decision.
- Some of you need to surrender your emotions at Jesus' feet.

The enemy wants to remove you from your place of destiny, but **God is calling you back to faithfulness**. Stay the course. Run your race. **Finish well.**

Closing Prayer

Heavenly Father, I come before You acknowledging the weight on my heart. I realize that I have considered leaving the place You assigned me because of offense, pain, or impatience. Forgive me for reacting out of emotion rather than seeking Your will. Lord, anchor me in Your truth. Remind me why I started this journey in the first place and reignite the passion I once had. I choose faithfulness over convenience. I choose endurance over retreat. Help me finish well, trusting that You will reward every act of obedience in due season. In Jesus' mighty name, Amen.

CHAPTER ELEVEN: THE BENEFITS OF FAITHFULNESS

Faithfulness Still Matters

Faithfulness is one of the most powerful virtues in the kingdom of God. It is not merely about showing up; it is about consistency, trustworthiness, and unwavering commitment—especially when challenges arise. Many admire the blessings of faithful men and women but forget that those blessings came because they **remained steadfast** during hard times.

Faithfulness is the difference between people who see the promises of God and those who merely dream of them. **It qualifies you for divine promotion.**

- **Matthew 25:21** – "Well done, good and faithful servant! You have been faithful with a few things; I will put you in charge of many things." (Faithfulness brings increase.)
- **1 Corinthians 4:2** – "It is required that those who have been given a trust must prove faithful." (God expects faithfulness from those He entrusts.)
- **Revelation 2:10** – "Be faithful until death, and I will give you the crown of life." (Faithfulness secures eternal rewards.)

Faithfulness is not about duty alone; it is also about **honor, perseverance, and obedience**.

Faithfulness Is Generational

Faithfulness does not affect only you—it affects **your children and their children**. Your choice to remain faithful or become unfaithful can influence generations to come.

- **Exodus 20:6** – "Showing love to a thousand generations of those who love me and keep my commandments."
- **Proverbs 20:7** – "The righteous who walks in his integrity—blessed are his children after him!"

When you remain faithful to God's assignment, your **lineage** inherits the blessings of your obedience. Conversely, unfaithfulness can create negative ripples through your descendants.

Ask yourself: will your children inherit blessings because you stayed faithful, or will they struggle because of the choices you made?

Sonship vs the Orphan Spirit

Faithfulness is the hallmark of a true son. **Sons do not abandon the house; they build it.** Many believers struggle with faithfulness because they have yet to embrace their identity as sons. Servants come and go, but sons remain.

- **Romans 8:15–16** – "The Spirit you received brought about your adoption to sonship. And by him we cry, 'Abba, Father.'" (A son stays connected to the Father.)
- **Galatians 3:26–29** – "For in Christ Jesus you are all sons of God, through faith." (Sonship is about inheritance, not mere participation.)
- **Ephesians 6:1–3** – "Honor your father and mother... so that it may go well with you and that you may enjoy long life on the earth." (Honor undergirds faithfulness.)

Marks of a True Son

- A son honors the father and receives from him.
- Honor is the currency that holds the father-son relationship together.
- Dishonor breeds pride, and pride leads to downfall.
- A true son is accountable, even when it's difficult.
- Homes without honor produce "bastards," and bastards produce wicked generations.
- Submission is obedience, even under hardship.

An **orphan spirit**, however, rejects accountability and often leads to rebellion.

Signs of an Orphan Spirit

- Struggles with submission.
- Rejects correction and avoids accountability.
- Fosters disloyalty and rebellion.
- Abandons the house when circumstances grow difficult.
- **John 8:35** – "A slave has no permanent place in the family, but a son belongs to it forever." (Sons remain; orphans run.)

The orphan spirit is dangerous because it keeps people wandering instead of inheriting.

Spiritual Inheritance

- **2 Kings 2:9–10** – "Elisha said, 'Let me inherit a double portion of your spirit.' Elijah replied, 'If you see me when I am taken from you, it will be yours—otherwise, it will not.'"
  Elisha's faithfulness to Elijah positioned him for a double portion. Had he left Elijah prematurely, he would have missed his inheritance.
- Disloyalty disconnects you from inheritance.
- Faithfulness in service yields an impartation of grace.
- Many lose their place because they depart before their moment of receiving.

Faithfulness and Leadership Responsibility

Faithfulness is even more crucial for **those in leadership** or in positions of responsibility. Shepherds cannot walk away from their flock without consequences:

- **Matthew 26:31** – "Strike the shepherd, and the sheep will be scattered." (When a leader falls or abandons their post, it affects everyone under them.)
- **Ezekiel 34:10** – "I am against the shepherds and will hold them accountable for my flock." (God takes shepherding seriously.)
- **Hebrews 13:17** – "Obey your leaders and submit to them, for they keep watch over your souls as those who will have to give an account." (Leaders are responsible for their people.)

If God has placed you in a leadership role, you do not have the same freedom to quit as others might. The moment you assume responsibility, **God holds you accountable** for the souls under your covering. Leaving in anger or frustration does not absolve you—it transfers the weight of failure to those who depended on your faithfulness.

"Once you say yes to the calling on your life, everything you do matters and can impact those you serve. Leaving incorrectly can harm the sheep and cause them to stumble. Leaders must exit with grace and clarity, ensuring an atmosphere that supports the flock's continued growth—even if the leader's season is ending."

Final Call: Stay the Course

Faithfulness is costly, but unfaithfulness costs even more.

- Do not let offense push you from your place of destiny.
- Do not walk away because you feel unseen—God sees you.
- Do not quit when your breakthrough could be right around the corner.

Remain faithful and stay the course. **Your reward is coming.**

- **Galatians 6:9** – "Let us not grow weary in doing good, for at the proper time we will reap a harvest if we do not give up."
- **Hebrews 6:10** – "God is not unjust; he will not forget your work and the love you have shown him."
- **1 Corinthians 15:58** – "Be steadfast, immovable, always abounding in the work of the Lord, knowing that your labor is not in vain."

Endure. Remain loyal. The fruit of faithfulness is a harvest of blessings, both for you and for generations yet to come.

CHAPTER TWELVE: TIME FOR A RESET

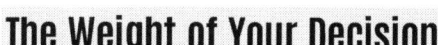

The Weight of Your Decision

Leaving a church is not a small decision. It isn't merely walking out of a building—it's a **spiritual shift**, a transition that carries consequences. It means leaving an environment that once fed you, stretched you, and refined you.

But consider this: **What if your desire to leave is not a call to exit, but a call to reset?**

You might be carrying **hurt, disappointment, exhaustion**—maybe you feel let down by leadership, or believe you've outgrown your current place. The easiest option is to walk away.

But pause:

- **Is your frustration being interpreted as God's direction?**
- **Is your exhaustion influencing your discernment?**
- **Is this truly a divine departure—or a reaction to unprocessed emotions?**

Many fail to realize they are **under spiritual attack** until they've already stepped out of alignment. Others ignore signs of **spiritual burnout**, thinking they can push through—until they collapse.

Hear this: **Burnout is dangerous. Offense is dangerous. Misalignment is dangerous.**

This is your **wake-up call**. Before you make a life-altering choice—**you need a reset**. A reset is neither weakness nor failure; it's a **divine strategy**.

Come back to clarity.
Come back to fire.
Come back to Me.

- **Isaiah 40:31** – "Those who wait on the Lord shall renew their strength…"
  (Perhaps what you need is not an exit but an encounter with fresh strength.)
- **Lamentations 3:22–23** – "Because of the Lord's great love we are not consumed… His mercies are new every morning."
  (If you think you've reached your limit, remember God's mercy resets daily.)
- **Psalm 51:10** – "Create in me a clean heart… and renew a right spirit within me."
  (Before you decide, let God transform your heart.)

This is not just about making yourself feel better; it's about ensuring that **you are not leaving a place God is still working on**.

The Silent Killers of Your Fire

Every believer will experience spiritual fatigue at some point. The enemy may not lure you into sin immediately, so he uses **subtle attacks**:

- **Spiritual depletion**: Have you been pouring out but never being refilled, confusing busyness with intimacy?
- **Unresolved wounds**: Are you silently hurting? Are you angry with God yet hiding it beneath a "deep" spirituality?
- **Loss of focus**: Has life's pressure distracted you from what God called you to do?

- **Misalignment**: Are you moving by divine instruction, or are you simply tired and reacting to it?
- **Compromise**: Have minor decisions gradually led you into lukewarmness, turning your hunger for God into mere obligation?

These silent killers will **choke your fire** if you do not reset in time.

Biblical Examples of a Reset

Even great men and women of God needed a divine reset:
- **Peter**: Denied Jesus and nearly returned to fishing, but Jesus restored his purpose (John 21:15–17).
- **Jonah**: Fled his calling, yet God gave him a second chance (Jonah 3:1–2).
- **Moses**: Spent 40 years in exile before God reset him to lead a nation (Exodus 3:10–12).

Your past mistakes, failures, or struggles **do not define you**. God is calling you back to power.

Before You Leave, Ask Yourself:

- **Am I leaving because I've outgrown this place, or because I'm spiritually weak right now?**
- **Have I truly given God space and time to speak before deciding?**
- **Am I making this choice from peace or from pain?**
- **Am I seeking the Holy Spirit's guidance, or am I following my emotions?**

If you haven't paused to reset, you risk making a **permanent decision** based on **temporary emotion**.

THE 7-DAY SPIRITUAL DETOX & RESET

A Call to Realignment, Refinement, and Revival

There comes a time in every believer's journey when they must step away from the noise, from the distractions, and from everything subtly weakening their hunger for God. In these moments, a divine reset is needed—a conscious return to the secret place, a repositioning under open heavens, and an invitation to a fresh outpouring of the Spirit.

This **7-Day Spiritual Reset Fast** is not a mere religious exercise—it is a divine invitation into deeper intimacy, spiritual realignment, and revival. By the end of these seven days, you will:

- Experience fresh encounters with God
- Break spiritual stagnation
- Rekindle a burning prayer life
- Silence distractions and sharpen your focus
- Walk in power, authority, and clarity

Approach it with expectation and consecration, knowing it is your **divine moment of realignment**.

DAY 1: RETURN TO YOUR FIRST LOVE

(Fast + Prayer & Meditation)

Scripture Reading:
Revelation 2:4–5 – "Yet I hold this against you: You have forsaken the

love you had at first. Consider how far you have fallen! Repent and do the things you did at first."

Returning to the Altar of Love

Many believers do not backslide overnight—it happens subtly. The fire that once burned fiercely becomes lukewarm, the urgency for God becomes casual, and the hunger that once drew you into deep encounters begins to fade. This first day is a call to return to your first love—to reignite the passion that once defined your walk with God.

FAST Instructions

- Commit to a water fast, fruit fast, or 6 AM–6 PM fast (as led by the Holy Spirit).
- Use meal times for worship and reflection.

Action Steps

1. **Remember the Fire** – Write down the moments that ignited your passion for God. Recall the last time you wept in His presence.
2. **Repent for Neglecting His Presence** – Confess any area where your hunger for Him has diminished.
3. **Pray for Restoration** – Ask the Holy Spirit to rekindle the flames of your love for God.

Prophetic Declarations for Day 1

- I decree that my heart returns to its first love for Jesus.
- Every distraction pulling me away from the presence of God is uprooted now.
- I hunger and thirst for righteousness; my soul longs for deeper encounters.

- The fire on my altar will never burn out—I am a dwelling place for God.
- Every spiritual coldness is consumed by fresh fire.
- I will love the Lord my God with all my heart, soul, and strength.
- I reject complacency and embrace divine passion for the things of the Spirit.
- I am not just a servant of God—I am a lover of His presence.
- Every substitute for God's presence in my life is removed in Jesus' name.
- I step into deeper intimacy with God; my heart is set ablaze for Him.

Closing Prayer for Day 1

Father, in the name of Jesus, I return to You with all my heart. I acknowledge that in the busyness of life, my pursuit of You has not been as it should. Forgive me for every moment I placed other things above my time with You. Lord, let my soul hunger again, let my spirit yearn again, and let my heart burn again for You.

Holy Spirit, rekindle the fire that once consumed me. Take me back to the place where prayer was my delight, where worship was my greatest pleasure, and where Your presence was my obsession. Remove every weight, distraction, and compromise that has dimmed my light. I break every cycle of spiritual laziness and inconsistency.

Lord, I ask for a new baptism of hunger. Let my heart chase after You like never before. Let my hands be lifted in surrender, my knees bow in reverence, and my lips declare Your praise. I refuse to be casual about my walk with You; I give You my full devotion.

I decree and declare that as I embark on this seven-day reset, my heart is fully turning to You. I silence every competing voice, and I declare that You alone are my desire. Let fresh fire fall. In Jesus' name, Amen.

DAY 2: BREAK SPIRITUAL HINDRANCES

(Fast + Deliverance Prayer)

Scripture Reading:
Hebrews 12:1 – "Let us throw off everything that hinders and the sin that so easily entangles."

Breaking the Chains That Weigh You Down

Spiritual dryness is often not accidental—baggage and hindrances weigh us down. Some are sinful, others are merely distractions, but all work against our pursuit of God. Day 2 is about exposing and eliminating anything pulling you away from the secret place.

FAST Instructions

- Continue your water/fruit/partial fast.
- Abstain from entertainment and unneeded conversations.

Action Steps

1. **Identify Three Spiritual Hindrances** – Write them down (secret sins, unhealthy relationships, or distracting habits).
2. **Pray Violently Against Them** – Renounce these hindrances with authority.
3. **Physically Remove Them** – If it's a habit, stop it today. If it's a toxic influence, cut it off immediately.

Prophetic Declarations for Day 2

- Every weight and sin slowing me down is broken in Jesus' name.
- I sever every soul tie that keeps me from the fullness of God.
- Every spiritual chain limiting my progress is shattered by fire.
- The blood of Jesus cleanses my mind, body, and spirit.
- I break free from every secret struggle; sin has no dominion over me.
- I walk in purity, holiness, and complete surrender to God's will.
- I reject every influence that contradicts my destiny in Christ.
- I am sanctified, purified, and set apart for divine purpose.
- No demonic oppression can hinder my spiritual growth.
- I declare total victory over every temptation and weakness in my life.

Closing Prayer for Day 2

Lord, I lay every weight at Your feet. I refuse to carry burdens never meant for me. I break free from distractions, sin, and every entanglement of the enemy. No longer will I struggle with the same issues—today I declare total freedom.

Father, expose every hidden area of my life that does not glorify You. Let Your refining fire purify my thoughts, actions, and desires. Where I have entertained compromise, cleanse me. Where I have justified disobedience, convict me.

I declare that from now on, nothing holds me back from my divine destiny. I walk in purity, in victory, and in the fullness of my calling. In Jesus' name, Amen.

DAY 3: REKINDLE THE PRAYER ALTAR

(Fast + One-Hour Prayer Session)

Scripture Reading:
Luke 18:1 – "Men ought always to pray and not faint."

Revival Begins on the Altar of Prayer

A believer's strength, power, and ability to navigate spiritual realms directly link to the strength of their prayer life. Prayer is not a religious activity—it is a channel for divine exchange and transformation. The enemy attacks your prayer life because **a prayerless Christian is a powerless Christian**.

FAST Instructions

- Continue your full or partial fast.
- Dedicate this day to prayer—avoid distractions.

Action Steps

1. **Commit to at Least One Hour of Prayer Today**
   - 20 min: Worship & Thanksgiving
   - 20 min: Intercession & Warfare
   - 20 min: Prophetic Declarations
2. **Pray in the Spirit for 30 Minutes**
   - If you have a prayer language, stir yourself by praying in tongues. Otherwise, ask the Holy Spirit to fill you.
3. **Remove Distractions** – Silence your phone and create an atmosphere for deep fellowship.

Prophetic Declarations for Day 3

- My prayer altar is on fire—I will not be silent before God.

- Every attack against my prayer life is destroyed in Jesus' name.
- I receive fresh oil for intercession and fresh grace for supplication.
- I am a watchman over my destiny, my family, and my generation.
- The heavens are open over my life—I hear God clearly and walk in the supernatural.
- I break free from prayerlessness and distractions.
- As I pray, angels are activated, burdens are lifted, and yokes are destroyed.
- I decree that my prayers bring acceleration, breakthroughs, and open doors.
- The fire of God consumes every form of weakness and coldness in my spirit.
- I receive the spirit of prayer and supplication—fresh passion rises within me.

Closing Prayer for Day 3

Father, I acknowledge that without prayer, I am powerless. Forgive me for allowing the cares of life to weaken my communion with You. I repent of inconsistency, distractions, and neglecting my altar. Today, I come with hunger.

Holy Spirit, ignite my prayer life. Let my spirit burn for intercession, let my lips declare Your mysteries, and let my heart beat with passion for Your presence. I ask for fresh fire that cannot be quenched.

Lord, I refuse to remain the same. I break out of dryness. As I press into prayer, I declare chains are breaking, doors are opening, and my spiritual senses are sharpening. Let my ears hear, let my eyes see into the realms of the Spirit.

From this moment, my life is an altar of prayer. I will stand in the secret place, tarry in Your presence, and partner with heaven. My life will reflect divine encounters. Let fresh fire fall upon me today, never to be lost again. In Jesus' name, Amen.

DAY 4: RENEW YOUR MIND

(Fast + Word Immersion)

Scripture Reading:
Romans 12:2 – "Do not conform to the pattern of this world, but be transformed by the renewing of your mind."

Your Mind Is a Battlefield—Win the War

A person's destiny is shaped by their thought patterns. You cannot walk in power, wisdom, and discernment if your mind is filled with worldly patterns, negative thinking, or toxic beliefs. Day 4 focuses on purging the mind of every contamination and immersing yourself in God's truth.

FAST Instructions
- Continue your fast.
- Eliminate worldly entertainment, social media, and unnecessary conversations for the day.

Action Steps
1. **Choose Three Scriptures That Counter the Lies You Have Believed**
   - If you struggle with fear, meditate on 2 Timothy 1:7.
   - If you struggle with insecurity, declare Psalm 139:14.
   - If you struggle with doubt, speak Jeremiah 29:11.

2. **Speak Them Aloud at Least Three Times Today**
3. **Limit External Noise** – No social media or unnecessary talk; let your mind soak in the Word.

Prophetic Declarations for Day 4

- My mind is renewed daily by God's Word.
- I reject every false belief that contradicts my destiny.
- I am not a victim—I am victorious through Christ.
- My thoughts align with the truth of God's Word.
- I cast down every imagination that exalts itself against the knowledge of Christ.
- I break free from toxic thought patterns and limiting mindsets.
- I walk in divine wisdom, understanding, and spiritual insight.
- My mind is fruitful, creative, and filled with God's ideas.
- I will not be conformed to the world, but transformed by the Word.
- As I meditate on Scripture, my faith grows, my confidence rises, and my destiny is secured.

Closing Prayer for Day 4

Father, I surrender my mind to You. My thought patterns shape my reality, and I desire to be fully aligned with Your truth. Every wrong mindset, every limiting belief, and every false perspective is broken in Jesus' name.

Lord, let Your Word wash me, cleanse me, and reprogram my thinking. I reject every lie of the enemy, embracing the truth of my identity in Christ. I am not a failure, I am not defeated, I am not bound—I am an overcomer.

Holy Spirit, saturate my thoughts with divine wisdom. Let my decisions, desires, and pursuits be governed by Kingdom principles. Remove every stronghold that prevents me from walking in power.

From this day on, my mind is renewed, my focus is sharp, and I am transformed by the living Word. I will meditate on truth, walk in wisdom, and manifest the mind of Christ. In Jesus' name, Amen.

DAY 5: STRENGTHEN ACCOUNTABILITY

(Fast + Fellowship & Prayer Call)

Scripture Reading:
Proverbs 27:17 – "As iron sharpens iron, so one person sharpens another."

You Cannot Walk This Journey Alone

Spiritual growth is not meant to be done alone. Many believers struggle because they try to sustain their fire in isolation. Divine alignment thrives in community. Day 5 focuses on strengthening godly relationships, seeking accountability, and surrounding yourself with those who sharpen you spiritually.

FAST Instructions
- Continue fasting as usual.
- Pray specifically for divine relationships.

Action Steps
1. **Reach Out to a Spiritual Mentor or Prayer Partner**
    - Identify one person who challenges and encourages your spiritual walk.

2. **Schedule a 10-Minute Prayer Call**
   - Pray with each other and keep each other accountable.
3. **Evaluate Your Inner Circle**
   - List the five closest people in your life. Do they push you toward God or pull you away?

Prophetic Declarations for Day 5

- I am surrounded by godly voices that sharpen my faith.
- I reject any relationship that pulls me away from my divine purpose.
- The Lord is sending men and women into my life who propel me into destiny.
- I receive the wisdom to build meaningful, spirit-led relationships.
- I am accountable, disciplined, and committed to growth.
- I break free from isolation; I will not walk alone in my faith.
- I receive the right mentors, leaders, and teachers for my spiritual journey.
- The wrong people exit my life, and the right people enter it.
- I will be sharpened, strengthened, and established through godly community.
- I decree that my destiny helpers locate me and my divine connections are secured.

Closing Prayer for Day 5

Father, I acknowledge I cannot walk this journey alone. Your Word says iron sharpens iron, so I ask You to align me with people who will strengthen my faith, challenge my walk, and propel me into destiny.

Lord, I renounce isolation and every spirit of pride that causes me to reject correction. I embrace divine accountability. Let my heart be humble, my spirit be teachable, and my relationships be godly.

Holy Spirit, remove every relationship hindering Your will. I declare I will no longer walk with those who drag me from Your presence. I am surrounded by wise counselors, guided by mentors, and supported by intercessors.

From now on, I walk in the path of the wise. I am surrounded by the right people, led by the right voices, and connected to those assigned to my future. In Jesus' mighty name, Amen.

DAY 6: FULL CONSECRATION

(Fast from Social Media, Entertainment & Distractions)

Scripture Reading:
Psalm 46:10 – "Be still, and know that I am God."

Shut Out the Noise, Tune Into Heaven

Fasting is not only about food—it's also about eliminating distractions so you can hear God clearly. Often, believers struggle to discern God's voice because they are too busy to listen. Today, step away from social media, entertainment, and unneeded conversations to immerse yourself in God's presence.

FAST Instructions
- No social media, TV, or other entertainment.
- Eliminate unnecessary conversations—focus on stillness before God.

Action Steps
1. **Spend Extended Time in Worship & Prayer**
    o Create a deep atmosphere for communion with God.
2. **Read a Full Chapter of the Bible Slowly**
    o Absorb every verse, letting the Word speak to you.
3. **Journal Everything God Speaks**
    o Expect revelation, instructions, and confirmations.

Prophetic Declarations for Day 6

- I silence every voice that is not of God.
- I receive divine clarity and direction for my destiny.
- Every spiritual blockage preventing me from hearing God is removed.
- I enter into divine encounters—my eyes are open to see what God reveals.
- My spirit is still before God, and I receive His instructions.
- I walk in supernatural wisdom and understanding.
- I declare my atmosphere consecrated and filled with God's presence.
- I reject distractions and worldly influences over my mind and heart.
- I dwell in the secret place of the Most High—God reveals His mysteries to me.
- My sensitivity to the Spirit is heightened—no more confusion, only clarity.

Closing Prayer for Day 6

Father, I come before You today with a heart longing to hear Your voice. I renounce every distraction, noise, and competing voice that has pulled me from intimacy with You. I silence the world and open my spirit to You.

Holy Spirit, speak to me. Let my heart be sensitive to Your whispers. Let my mind be focused, my soul be still. I declare that my ears are open to divine instructions and my eyes open to spiritual realities.

Lord, remove every activity, person, or habit that robs me of Your presence. I consecrate myself fully—spirit, soul, and body. I will not trade divine encounters for worldly distractions.

From now on, I walk in stillness before You. I cultivate an atmosphere of Your presence and dwell in deep communion with You. Let my life be a sanctuary for Your glory. In Jesus' name, Amen.

DAY 7:
PROPHETIC DECLARATIONS & FINAL COVENANT WITH GOD

(Fast + Personal Commitment)

Scripture Reading:
Job 22:28 – "You shall decree a thing, and it shall be established for you."

Seal Your Reset in Prophecy

Today is not a day of requests—it's a day of establishing your spiritual realignment in the heavens and on earth. It is a day of alignment, consecration, and covenant. Every stronghold that has been broken will not return. Every revelation received is activated. Every transformation started remains permanent.

FAST Instructions
- Maintain your chosen fast.
- End the day with gratitude and thanksgiving.

Action Steps
1. **Speak Bold Prophetic Declarations Over Your Life** – This is the day of divine establishment.
2. **Write a Personal Covenant With God** – Declare your commitment to remain aligned.
3. **Celebrate Your Reset** – Offer thanksgiving and worship, confident that your life will never be the same.

Prophetic Declarations for Day 7

Isaiah 55:11 – "So shall My word be that goes forth from My mouth; it shall not return to Me void…"

- I decree this spiritual reset is permanent.
- Every stronghold that was broken will not return.
- I walk in divine clarity, discernment, and supernatural wisdom.
- The fire on my altar remains—I will not grow cold again.
- I am aligned with God's will—no more distractions or confusion.
- My hunger for the Word of God is unquenchable—revelation flows in my life.
- I am divinely connected to the right people—destiny helpers locate me now.
- Every door that was once closed is now open—favor follows me.
- I walk in purity, holiness, and consecration.
- I will fulfill my purpose—nothing can derail me from my calling.
- The hand of God rests upon me—I walk in divine power and authority.

- My life is a testimony of transformation—my past no longer defines me.
- I move forward in faith, strength, and complete victory.
- I am planted in the house of the Lord—I will not be uprooted.
- From today, my life is marked by encounters, breakthroughs, and supernatural acceleration.

(Pray in the Spirit for at least 15 minutes to seal these declarations.)

Final Covenant With God

Psalm 25:14 – "The Lord confides in those who fear Him; He makes His covenant known to them."

A covenant is an unbreakable agreement between you and God. Today, write your personal commitment to remain aligned, consecrated, and surrendered to His will.

Suggested Prompts:
1. **Maintain the Prayer Altar** – How will you remain consistent in prayer?
2. **Pursue Purity** – Outline how you will guard your heart and mind against offense or sin.
3. **Discipline Your Mind** – Identify what you will avoid and how you will meditate on God's Word daily.
4. **Obey Promptly** – Pledge to obey God's instructions without hesitation.
5. **Never Return to Bondage** – Declare that you will not revert to old chains; your freedom is permanent.

Numbers 23:19 – "God is not a man, that He should lie… Has He said, and will He not do?"

Final Closing Prayer for Day 7

Father, in the name of Jesus, I stand before You today in complete surrender. I thank You for the work You have done in my spirit, mind, and body throughout these seven days of consecration. Without You, I am nothing, but in You, I have all things.

Lord, I declare that every transformation is permanent. Every bondage broken will not return. Every renewed mindset will not revert to old patterns. Every spiritual hindrance is dismantled, and I walk forward in absolute freedom.

Father, thank You for the fresh hunger birthed in me. I will not allow the cares of life to weaken my fire again. My prayer altar remains ablaze, my love for Your Word stays strong, and my pursuit of Your presence never wanes. I will be found faithful.

I take authority over every plan of the enemy to sabotage this reset. Satan, you have lost. I am no longer bound, distracted, or weighed down. The blood of Jesus seals my victory, and I walk in supernatural alignment.

Holy Spirit, I ask for grace to maintain this momentum. Help me stay disciplined in prayer, consistent in study, and faithful in my assignment. I declare my life will be a reflection of Your glory. Everywhere I go, I will shine as a burning lamp in the midst of darkness.

Thank You, Lord, for this new beginning. I will never be the same. I am transformed, empowered, and victorious. In the mighty name of Jesus, Amen.

Your Reset Is Complete—Now Walk In It

This is not the end; it is the beginning of a new season. Stay accountable, remain disciplined, and stay on fire for God. Write down how you will maintain your spiritual growth, making it a lifelong commitment. Continue in alignment, stay hungry, and watch God do mighty exploits through your life.

CHAPTER THIRTEEN: IT'S TIME TO GO!

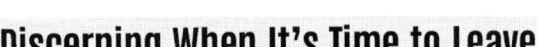

Discerning When It's Time to Leave

Not every departure from a church is wrong, and not every stay is right. There comes a point when remaining in a place **hinders your spiritual growth and destiny**. Leaving a church is a serious decision—one that must be done with **wisdom, prayer, and divine order**.

Many have left prematurely out of offense, misunderstanding, or rebellion, while others have stayed too long in toxic environments that stunted their growth. The key is discerning when God is truly saying, "It's time to go."

- **Ecclesiastes 3:1** – "To everything there is a season, and a time to every purpose under heaven."
  (God moves in seasons, and sometimes He shifts us.)

- **Isaiah 43:19** – "See, I am doing a new thing… Do you not perceive it?"
  (When God is moving, you must have the sensitivity to see it.)

- **1 Corinthians 14:40** – "Let everything be done decently and in order."
  (Leaving should be done with honor, not in rebellion or chaos.)

This chapter will help you **navigate a God-led transition**, ensuring that your exit is not based on emotions but on divine direction.

When Is It Truly Time to Leave?

There are **right** and **wrong** reasons to leave a church. Some depart for the wrong reasons—offense, impatience, or misunderstandings—while others ignore clear signs that God is calling them to move forward.

Signs That It May Be Time to Leave

1. **Doctrinal Deviation**
   The church has begun **teaching false doctrine** that contradicts the Bible. If the Word is compromised, your spiritual health is at risk.

2. **Spiritual Abuse**
   Leadership is **manipulative, controlling, or authoritarian**, using fear and guilt instead of love and grace. God does not call His people to be oppressed.

3. **No Spiritual Growth**
   You find yourself **stagnant, disconnected, or spiritually dry**, despite earnestly seeking growth.

4. **Toxic Environment**
   The church is rife with **gossip, slander, power struggles, and division**, making it hard to focus on God's presence.

5. **Unrepentant Moral Corruption in Leadership**
   Ongoing sin in leadership is **covered up rather than corrected**, revealing deep spiritual decay.

6. **God's Direct Instruction**
   Through **prayer, prophetic confirmation, and godly counsel**, you sense your assignment in this house is ending. This should not stem from frustration or personal ambition, but from a **consistent leading** of the Holy Spirit.

But What If God Wants You to Stay and Be Part of the Solution?

It's important to note that sometimes God does not want you to leave—even when you see corruption, compromise, or conflict. Instead, He may be positioning you to be an answer within the house.

Consider **Nathan the prophet**. When King David sinned, Nathan did not leave his position in frustration or disgust. He was assigned to confront David's sin and call him to repentance. If Nathan had run away, David might have remained in wrongdoing, leading Israel into further moral decline (2 Samuel 12:1-14).

By contrast, **Ahithophel**, David's counselor, was offended by David's actions and eventually walked away from his assignment. Instead of confronting the issue or staying to restore honor, he aligned with Absalom's rebellion and took his own life (2 Samuel 17:23).

- **Nathan's obedience** brought restoration.
- **Ahithophel's offense** led to destruction.

Not every difficult season in a church is a sign to leave. Sometimes, God is calling you to stand, to intercede, to correct, and to be a voice of righteousness. The questions to ask are:

- **Are you running from a challenge God wants you to face?**
- **Are you abandoning a place where God has called you to bring change?**
- **Is this truly a departure, or is it a divine assignment to stand firm?**

Discern wisely. There is a time to exit and a time to engage. Leaving without clarity may mean abandoning a place where God has assigned you as a solution.

Have You Been Bitten by a Serpent?

One of the greatest dangers in any church is not just what happens in the pulpit, but **what happens in the shadows**. Some people leave not because of their own experiences, but because they were **poisoned** by **whispers, slander, and manipulation.**

There are serpents in the church—agents of division and deception who seldom leave themselves, yet work behind the scenes to make others depart.

- They appear loyal to leadership but criticize them behind closed doors.
- They plant seeds of doubt, making you question what you once loved about your church.
- They mask themselves in spirituality, but their words carry venom.
- They always have "inside information" yet never solutions.
- They turn faithful people against leadership while staying close to leadership themselves.

This tactic is **not** new; it began in Eden when the serpent manipulated Eve to **distrust God** (Genesis 3:1–5). **Judas** sat among Jesus' disciples yet **undermined Him** (Luke 22:3–6).

Have You Been Poisoned?

- Did you suddenly become critical of leadership based on gossip rather than personal experience?
- Has your passion for serving waned after spending time with certain people?
- Do you feel "more enlightened" but also more disconnected?

That's how serpents operate: **they shift your perspective before pushing you out of alignment.**

Prayer: "Lord, if I have been poisoned by a serpent's words, cleanse me! Uproot every seed of dishonor and deception. Realign my heart with Your truth. Let me see clearly again. In Jesus' name, Amen."

Wrong Reasons for Leaving a Church

Many leave **not** because God sent them, but because their emotions pushed them out.

- **Offense & Hurt Feelings**
  Someone offended you, and instead of addressing it biblically (Matthew 18:15–17), you left.

- **Lack of Recognition**
  You felt unnoticed, and your desire for a platform eclipsed your desire for purpose.

- **Impatience**
  God's process took too long, so you sought to accelerate your own promotion.

- **Church Discipline**
  You faced correction but refused to repent, choosing to flee accountability.

- **Comparison & Covetousness**
  Another church looked more appealing, and you moved without asking if God was leading you.

How to Leave in Honor & Wisdom

If God has truly released you, how you leave matters **as much** as the decision to leave. Some depart in rebellion and gossip, unknowingly **closing doors** to future blessings and relationships. Leaving properly is a **test of character and maturity**.

1. Seek God's Direction & Confirm Your Release

- Leaving is serious; do not decide based on impulse or frustration.
- Pray and fast for clarity.
- Seek wise counsel from spiritually mature believers not entangled in your offense (Proverbs 11:14).
- If only disgruntled people confirm your choice, be cautious—offense might be steering you.

Ask yourself:

- Am I deciding this in God's presence or from frustration?
- Has God confirmed my release more than once, or am I seeking an excuse to leave?
- Have I let God purify my heart of offense, bitterness, and ambition?

2. Communicate with Leadership Directly & Respectfully

- Do not "ghost" the church. Request a meeting with your pastor or leader.
- Speak humbly and honestly. If concerns need addressing, do so with **honor** (1 Thessalonians 5:12–13).
- **What NOT to say**: "This church doesn't feed me anymore," or "God told me to leave, I owe no explanation," or "I just don't feel connected."
- **What to say instead**: "I've been seeking God about my next season, and I feel led to transition. I appreciate everything I've received here."

If leadership reacts poorly, bless them anyway. Their response is **their** test, not yours.

Why this matters: How you exit one season dictates how you enter the next. Leaving in anger or pride sets you up for repetitive cycles.

3. Avoid Gossip, Slander & Division

- Do not speak against the church or its leadership once you're gone.
- Refrain from venting frustrations to other members or spreading offense (Ephesians 4:29).
- If people ask why you left, answer graciously.

What NOT to do:

- "That pastor doesn't hear from God—that's why I left."
- "That church is hypocritical—I had to bail out."

What to say instead:

- "I left because God is leading me to a new season, and I'm grateful for all I received there."
- "Every church has strengths and weaknesses, but my time there has ended. I'm following God's lead."

Why this matters: Gossip invites curses (Proverbs 6:16–19), and slander about your former spiritual covering can close doors to future assignments.

4. Serve Until the End & Leave a Blessing

- Do not depart abruptly. If you served in ministry, allow time for a proper handover.
- Train your replacement if needed; this shows maturity and honors the church.
- Bless the church with words and prayers before you go.

Why this matters: Leaving in honor, integrity, and faithfulness keeps you under God's favor. You do not curse the very place that once fed you.

5. Find a New Church with God's Guidance

- Do not wander aimlessly. Some leave and spend years without spiritual covering.
- Your next step should be about **assignment**, not comfort.
- Ask God: "Where do You want me next? How can I serve and remain accountable?"

Why this matters: Isolation makes you vulnerable (Hebrews 10:25). Outside divine alignment, you become an easy target for the enemy.

6. Release & Forgive Before Moving On
- If you're leaving due to hurt, forgive before you depart.
- Offense carried into your next season poisons new relationships.
- Pray for your former church as an act of obedience (Matthew 6:14–15).

Why this matters: Forgiveness is not about feeling—it's about freeing your heart from bitterness.

Prayer: "Lord, I release every hurt, offense, and expectation. I bless my former church and thank You for what I received there. I move forward in peace, joy, and clarity. In Jesus' name, Amen."

The Consequences of Leaving Poorly

Leaving a church without divine order may lead to spiritual fallout:

1. **Spiritual Wandering**
   Many wander from church to church, struggling to find covering (Hebrews 10:25).
2. **Lost Opportunities**
   Leaving in rebellion may forfeit relationships and mentorship God intended for your growth (Proverbs 27:17).

3. **Bitterness & Unresolved Wounds**
   Departing without forgiving or releasing the past means old wounds follow you (Matthew 6:14–15).

Final Charge: Leaving in Alignment with God's Will

- I will not leave my place of destiny prematurely.
- I will not be ruled by offense, but by the wisdom of God.
- I refuse to move without divine instruction—I am led by the Spirit.
- I leave with honor, move in peace, and step into my new season with clarity.

If God truly says it's time to go, **go in peace and integrity**—leaving a trail of blessings rather than wounds. Your obedience will open new doors of favor, and your honor will protect your future. Run your race **in alignment** with His will.

FINAL WORDS & CONCLUSION

A Call to Reflection

As you turn these final pages, pause to reflect. This journey has not just been about identifying the struggles that drive people away from the church—it has been about revealing the deeper truths of **faithfulness, endurance, and divine alignment.**

You have encountered the Hopper, the Blamer, the Attention Seeker, the Abused, the Rejected, the Bleeding Leader, the Confused, the Independent Spirit, and the Offended. Each represents **real challenges** faced within the body of Christ. Yet through every story and every teaching, one constant remains:

- **God desires faithfulness** over fleeting passion.
- **God rewards endurance** over comfort.
- **God calls us to maturity,** not convenience.

The decision to stay or leave must never be taken lightly. Whether you've wrestled with offense, burnout, confusion, or disappointment, the ultimate question remains:

Will you endure? Will you fight for your faith? Will you stay planted until God Himself directs otherwise?

Before You Leave - Ask Yourself

Before making a life-altering choice about your church, ministry, or faith, carefully consider:

1. Am I leaving because of temporary frustration, or is God truly leading me?
2. Have I sought wise counsel from mature, unbiased believers?
3. Have I forgiven those who hurt me, ensuring my heart is free from offense?
4. Have I been faithful in small things, or am I abandoning my post because events didn't match my expectations?
5. Am I moving to a place where I can keep growing, or am I running from needed correction?

A decision made hastily or in heightened emotion can bring lasting consequences. Seek God's presence, His confirmation, and His wisdom before taking your next step.

Remain Steadfast

Faithfulness is the mark of spiritual maturity. Quitting is easy when challenges arise, but true sons and daughters of the Kingdom stand firm unless God uproots them.

- **Galatians 6:9** – "Let us not grow weary in doing good, for in due season we shall reap if we do not give up."
- **James 1:12** – "Blessed is the one who perseveres under trial… that person will receive the crown of life."
- **Hebrews 6:12** – "We do not want you to become lazy, but to imitate those who through faith and patience inherit what has been promised."

I decree and declare that I will remain faithful until my due season arrives!
I will not allow offense, weariness, or confusion to push me out of my divine assignment!
I receive grace to endure, to mature, and to walk in wisdom!
I refuse to be counted among those who start well but fail to finish!
I will flourish where God has planted me and reap the full harvest of my obedience!

Closing Prayer

"Lord, I surrender my will to You. Grant me wisdom to discern my season and strength to remain faithful. Keep me from moving outside Your timing. If I must stay, give me endurance to serve well. If I must leave, let it be with honor and divine direction. May my journey be a testimony of steadfast faith. In Jesus' name, Amen."

A Word of Encouragement

If you have been struggling—feeling forgotten, unseen, or weary—know this: **God sees you.** Your labor is not in vain, and your faithfulness will be rewarded. Do not let temporary discomfort bring permanent misalignment. Stay in His will, stay faithful, and stay planted unless He directs you otherwise.

Your destiny is greater than your emotions. Your reward is greater than your struggle. And your faithfulness does not go unnoticed by the One who both calls and sustains you.

Stay the course. **Finish well.**

Printed in Poland
by Amazon Fulfillment
Poland Sp. z o.o., Wrocław